Bethany Lutheran Church
West Branch, Iowa

P9-ARM-177

GROWING UP
IS A
FAMILY AFFAIR

GROWING UP
IS A
FAMILY AFFAIR

by

ETHEL L. HERR

MOODY PRESS

CHICAGO

© 1978 by
THE MOODY BIBLE INSTITUTE
OF CHICAGO

All rights reserved. No part of this book may be reproduced
in any form without permission in writing from the publisher,
except in the case of brief quotations embodied in critical
articles or reviews.

All Scripture quotations, except those noted otherwise, are
from the *New American Standard Bible,* © 1960, 1962, 1963,
1968, 1971, 1972, 1973, and 1975, by The Lockman Foundation, and are used by permission.

Library of Congress Cataloging in Publication Data

Herr, Ethel L
  Growing up is a family affair.

  1. Herr, Ethel L. 2. Parent and child—Biography.
3. Family—United States. I. Title.

HQ535.H46   301.42'7   78-17581

ISBN 0-8024-3357-X

The use of selected references from various versions of the
Bible in this publication does not necessarily imply publisher
endorsement of the versions in their entirety.

Moody Paperback Edition, 1982
2 3 4 5 6 Printing/GB/Year 87 86 85 84 83 82

Printed in the United States of America

Dedication

Dear Kids,

You're growing up so very fast.
In umpteen ways we take your measure:
First tooth
            first step
                        first day of school
Each "first" brings parental pleasure.
Sheepskin
            driving permit
                        license to wed
Each document becomes a family treasure.

Our rate of growth is slower,
And you must judge from subtler indications:
Patience
            kindness
                        sensitivity
Virtues that build strong foundations
Loyalty
            self-control
                        consistency
Values that help meet God's expectations.

Oh, please
Remember, when we fail
(as often so do you)
Be patient with us, Kids,
For we are growing too.
            Love,
                        Mom and Dad

Contents

Preface

Growing up is a lifetime journey. Beginning in the cradle and continuing through hundreds of stages, it leads us via the grave into eternity, where its final outcome can scarcely be imagined. "Man was made for maturity," wrote E. Stanley Jones. But he could claim no originality for his idea. The apostle Paul had it centuries earlier: "We are meant to . . . grow up in every way into Christ" (Ephesians 4:15, Phillips*).

The pages of history abound with examples of men and women and children interacting with each other, with their environments, and with God in the constant pursuit of maturity. Because God is infinitely creative, He's made His human creatures into diverse individuals. Hence, He uses a wide variety of means to assist us in this lifelong process of maturing.

To parents He has given a special group of teachers that do a fantastic job if we give them half a chance. I'm speaking of our children.

My husband and I entered parenthood with high ideals and a noble sense of mission. For our motto we took the Bible admonition to "train up a child in the way he should go: and when he is old, he will not depart from it" (Proverbs 22:6, KJV) . We expected through discipline, example, and consistent training to raise a family of dedicated Christians. These we defined as adults whose pathway of life paralleled our own, at least in religious matters.

Convinced of the proverbial truth "As the twig is bent,

*J. B. Phillips, *The New Testament in Modern English.*

9

so grows the tree," we recognized our function to be the bending of the twigs. We gave little consideration to our own need to bend and grow. Like older, stronger trees in a forest, we felt we stood tall enough to see what life was all about.

Over the years our attitudes have changed. Our failures have humbled us. Successes have pointed us in new directions. Seeing ourselves as immature and needing growth has helped us to put the children in a better perspective. No longer do we look upon them as trainees but as persons. We have learned not only to extend parental love to them but to like and appreciate them for the intriguing persons they are.

What has made the difference and changed our viewpoint? Many factors have contributed, of course. However most of the credit belongs to our children themselves, for in living with an active, growing family, we too have found ourselves being bent. In dozens of compelling ways, our little teachers have taught us that the goal of parenthood is not to reproduce ourselves in carbon-copy models of Christian virtue. Rather, the goal of the family is maturity for each individual and for the family as a living, growing unit. In the words of one friend's mother, "We raise our children to give them wings."

Parenting can become the most frustrating and disappointing venture of our lives, or it can bring us rewarding fulfillment and joy beyond our wildest dreams. My husband and I have sampled both experiences, and we've concluded that our attitude toward and reaction to parenthood hinges on how well we manage to accept our children in their dual role of learners and teachers.

I'm not writing this book because we've found a gold mine of answers to pass on to the world. Nor can I yet say we've successfully raised three children and launched them into acceptable Christian adulthood.

I'm writing this book because we've discovered that, through all the frustrations and joys, parenting can be fun. And we want to share with you some of the excitement we experience as our children are helping us grow. We want to show you a bit of the parenting glow these youngsters have returned to our lives, since we began to recognize them as our companions on the long journey toward maturity.

1

Growing Up Is a Family Affair

The November I turned twenty-five, I felt quite mature and self-confident. After all, I had traveled two thousand miles by train, had spent a hot summer alone on the East Coast, and, accompanied by our three small children, three years old and under, had made the long, trans-Atlantic flight to the Netherlands.

Such adventures demanded maturity (or at least produced it), I reasoned. Following my Air Force husband, I had spent all my married life on the go. But one strong force stabilized me through the confusion of mobility—a deep desire to help my children *grow up* and find their place in God's plan.

By spring, however, I learned that I had some growing up to do myself.

Reader's Digest called that winter Europe's worst in fifty years. Our native California bloodstreams confirmed the verdict. An accumulation of ice and snow deepened on our front lawn until three-year-old Martha finally asked, "When will this Christmas snow go away? I want to see the grass!"

At first my husband, Walt, and I accepted the new challenges with typical youthful enthusiasm. We found it almost fun learning to cook on coal heaters to avoid a deep-freeze kitchen, where dishcloths froze to the drainboard, and ice crystals formed in detergent bottles overnight. Snuggled under our electric blanket at night we looked with some semblance of delight at Jack Frost's icy etchings on the inside of bedroom windows. And what could be more beautiful than those breathtaking Saturday-morning drives through the magical world of ice-laden tree branches?

But winter's face turned decidedly gray each time the coal man arrived. Pouring fifty dollars a month into two greedy coal heaters to warm the fifteen-foot ceiling of our oversized living room never remotely resembled fun. I tried with little success to convince myself that climbing two flights of stairs to wash endless loads of diapers in the family bathtub would keep my figure trim.

We lived in a Dutch village and had almost no English-speaking neighbors for miles around. For four gloomy months, the cold, the distance from our few American friends, and a bad bout of the flu confined us to our living-dining room area. We felt like prisoners, locked away behind a huge mahogany door and four uninsulated brick walls.

As the days grew grayer and our confinement lengthened, pressures mounted, and tempers shortened. With increasing frequency the children's pent-up energies exploded. The rosy glow of adventure slid out of sight over the horizon of our tomorrows. In its place, coal-dusted walls and dingy green draperies closed in on me.

One awful morning in March, bitterness and frustration threatened to win the battle over my spirit. Toys cluttered the living room floor. Heaps of this and that lay everywhere. Two toddlers quarreled in the midst of the mess. Only one tiny corner bespoke peace. In her crib, near the brink of sleep, the baby lay drinking a late morning bottle.

As I pinned my daily dozen diapers to the flimsy wire clothesline hooked over the hall door, I wanted to shout: Diapers, diapers, diapers! Is there nothing in life but these dingy, nasty diapers?

Instead I suppressed the urge, and took out my fury physically on the soggy muslin rectangles. I jerked them from their basket and pulled at them with angry movements.

Then, just as one-year-old Mary Jane slipped off to sleep, two-year-old Tim vented his anger by hitting three-year-old Martha over the head with the plastic hammer he had gotten for Christmas. His big sister instantly retaliated with a wail, and a shove that sent her chubby brother sprawling to the floor.

Why this fight should upset me so, I didn't know. After all, I had been serenaded all morning long by the background music of their quarreling. But something inside me exploded. Emotions cried louder than reason. By turns, I grabbed each child by a heavily sweatered shoulder and plunked both into overstuffed chairs at opposite corners of the room.

"But, Mommie, he hit me first," Martha protested.

"I don't care who did what first, or how, or why," I snapped.

Pouting, Tim defended himself. "She tried to bossy me."

"Keep still while I'm talking to you," I ordered.

Martha began to cry. "And stop that blubbering. I've heard all the crybaby stuff and fighting I'm going to take for one day. Do you hear?" My voice escalated with each sentence until I shouted, "I've had it with you two! If there's one more fight, you're both going to get the hardest spanking you've ever had in your lives!"

Returning to the half-empty clothes basket, I barked one last command: "Now you just sit there until I tell you to get down. And not a sound from either one of you. Not a sound!"

Grousing, I bent down to pick up a tiny undershirt. *Will they ever grow up?* Not until I held the tiny garment in my fingers did I notice that both of my hands were trembling. Next my whole body began to shake, and unexpected tears spilled onto my cheeks.

Past several rows of wet diapers, I fumbled frantically for the door handle and hurried into the huge, echoey hallway. *My children mustn't see me cry.* I leaned against a massive banister and prayed a desperate prayer: *O God, what's the matter with me? I used to be the girl without a temper. Remember? Now, here I am spouting out more anger in one winter than I've ever produced in my whole life.*

My knees sagged shakily, and my fingers formed a mass of white knuckles around the banister. *I just lose control of myself when it hits me this way. God, I'm scared of what I might do to these children.*

There, against the rail, I cried myself dry. Finally, feeling calm but exhausted, I imagined how I would have acted if my mother had been here. I knew I would have restrained myself. Self-control always came easy when I tried to show her what a good mother I was.

Could it be that my mature self-control depended on the presence of my mother?

Impossible. I was no child.

A baby's sudden wail from the other room wrenched me back to the dismal present. Wiping my eyes and blowing my nose, I thought, *What a childish mess I am.*

Moments later I lifted the baby from her crib, then turned to the two prisoners in their chairs. "You may get down now." I spoke softly, almost fearing my own voice. "And no more fussing, unless you want to go back."

I watched them return to their play on the paper-strewn carpet. Seeming to have forgotten the former nasty scene, they began to play peacefully.

I set the baby down on the floor with the others, and wondered why I had reached this miserable crisis. Was it really an emotional reaction to a severe winter in a foreign country? Or did it have other roots?

A dim scene from memory began to come into focus in my confused mind. I had returned to the maternity ward of a California hospital just a year before. The night nurse, a heavyset Christian woman in her early forties, took my temperature, fluffed my pillows, administered bedtime medication. All the while she shared with me her personal testimony.

"I've known the Lord Jesus since my teens." She smiled and added with a twinkle in her eye, "That's quite awhile! But to this day, every time I open my Bible, I make some thrilling discovery."

Understanding and agreeing, I nodded. Not too many years before I too had experienced this sort of enthusiasm for my faith. But inside, an honest recognition jolted me. Somewhere among the kitchen pots and laundry pails, I'd lost it.

That night, in a moment of strong yearning, I had begged God to help me recapture that invigorating zest for life.

Now, as I donned a bulky knit sweater and headed for the kitchen to fix lunch, I wondered, *Could that longing I felt a year ago in Emmanuel Hospital have anything to do with this frustration I suffer today?*

Mechanically I opened a soup can and sliced the fresh bread, delivered hot at the door an hour earlier. Warm tears dribbled down my cheeks once more, as I prayed, *O God, I need Your help. I've prayed and prayed for weeks about my worsening temper. But You haven't answered.*

Spreading cold, hard butter on a slice of warm whole-wheat bread, I went on: *Just now, though, I think I'm beginning to get the idea. Is it because first You had to show me that my temper is only one symptom of the real disease— the same disease You tried to tell me about a year ago? Immaturity, maybe? Yes, Lord, You heard me right. I said immaturity.*

That afternoon I relaxed with my children for the first time since winter had imprisoned us behind the heavy, mahogany doors of this barnlike ghost of a mansion. I read "and-they-all-lived-happily-ever-after" storybooks and helped build tumble towers with three *delightful* toddlers.

In the process I began to suspect that my children were the teachers God was using to show me how immature I was. It had taken them a whole gray winter of frustrating experiences, not because they were poor teachers (actually, they were the best), but because I seem to be a terribly slow learner.

The years that have followed have comprised one continuing adventure. For, in the ups and downs and ins and outs of daily living, my children have been helping both their father and me recognize and deal with dozens of unsuspected pockets of emotional and spiritual immaturity in ourselves. Together, as a family, we've all learned to delight in the truth that growing up in Christ is a family affair, in which the children often star as teachers.

Part 1

LOVING LIFE: AN APPROACH TO GROWTH

On an ordinary November morning, I went about my duties in my tiny, high-ceilinged kitchen. Through the long, narrow windows, the typically overcast sky shed its spell of dullness over my routine.

My insignificant thoughts were interrupted when our preschool daughter darted across the backyard and burst through the door.

"Mommy, look!" Martha waved before my face a handful of bright yellow and orange leaves, and shouted: "In the alley pathway, I found fall!"

Suddenly the day ceased to be ordinary. This one, brief encounter with childlike insight and enthusiasm set that day apart as something colorful and rare in my memory album.

Many times throughout my mothering years, my children have accosted me in a mundane mood and proclaimed that life is much too exhilarating to be spoiled with negative attitudes. Over and over they have worked to convince me that growing up means fully living life by loving it.

And their idea is scriptural. In Deuteronomy 16:11, I read that Moses encouraged

19

God's people to live life in this way. "You
shall rejoice before the LORD your God, you
and your son and your daughter . . . in the
place where the LORD your God chooses to establish His name."

Today, we're learning along with many families, that growth begins with positive, rejoic-
ing attitudes. In Part 1 of this book, we'll
share some of these attitudes and how in our
family the divinely appointed teacher-children
have helped us to develop them.

Defining maturity as our primary goal and
living with enthusiasm, childlikeness, adaptability, room for questions, and mutual confidence—all these have blended together in our
experience to prove that loving life is a workable approach to growing up.

2

What Is Growing Up?

One evening at bedtime, three-year-old Martha, wearing my bedroom slippers, shuffled into the living room. She grinned exultantly and announced: "See, Mommy—I'm a woman!"

Walt and I chuckled. We knew it took more than bedroom slippers to make a woman out of this imaginative child. But we also sensed a deeper message in her amusing pronouncement. To become a woman and a "mommy" (the two were synonymous to her) was the highest goal she could conceive. That was growing up at its arriving level. She demonstrated this in daily speech, by constantly talking of being "big old enough" to play with safety pins, to sew on Mommy's sewing machine, to wear high-heeled shoes.

Later Tim, at three, followed his daddy under the car, into the workshop, behind the lawn mower, and fixed all the toy trucks in his growing fleet. Mary Jane, at the same age, mothered and nursed all her baby dolls and little playmates.

We glowed with parental pride to think that these little people were aiming to arrive where we were. To the minds of our imitative children, we adults represented excellence. In our youthful inexperience, we let their parent worship feed our egos a bit, and enjoyed the new power parenthood had brought us. Not that we thought we were perfect. We knew ourselves too well to believe this. But we did feel confident that we were finally quite mature.

21

What was maturity to us back in those early days? Probably we hadn't defined it too well. I know I had always understood maturity to be largely a spiritual virtue. I felt this was the intent of Christ's command: "Be ye therefore perfect [often translated *mature*], even as your Father which is in heaven is perfect [mature]" (Matthew 5:48, KJV).

However, functioning at the practical levels of responsibility in the family circle opened my eyes to a broader meaning of these words. Each day I found myself facing the challenges of balancing parental authority with tact and respect, planning meals and schedules, nursing sick babies, trying to meet the physical and emotional needs of a husband and three demanding children.

I soon began to see how closely Jesus connected His call to perfection with a constant call to social maturity. I discovered He was saying that everyday matters of kindness and good ethics—feeding the hungry and healing the sick—were the flesh and blood manifestations of inner spiritual maturity. As a family we have been living with these realities ever since, and we are concluding that you cannot have one kind of maturity without the other.

Thirteen years after the bedroom slipper happening, Martha suggested to me, "Let's not grow old without growing up."

I wondered then how much she understood. Did she say "let's" because she had observed that maturity takes place in families—that we grow *together*, share ideas *together*, succeed *together*, fail *together*, pick each other up and go on *together?*

At least she was recognizing the possibility of never becoming mature—a tragedy she intended to avoid. I like to think we're all becoming aware that our highest goal is maturity for each individual and for our family as a unit. In the free exchange of aspirations and ideas our family enjoys, we talk about how far we all have to go. At times, this means confronting one another directly with the truth about our immaturities. Quite often we, the parents, are the confronted ones, and not just the confronters.

By nature, I am a bossy person. When I tell the children a thing, I usually tell them again, then repeat it once more for good measure. This had led to a good many confrontations, especially as the children began growing out of childhood.

I recall one occasion when I had delivered to Tim an emotion-packed lecture ending with a barbed challenge. Not being one to retaliate easily, the boy rushed off to his room.

Walt, who had overheard my bossy tirade, slipped his arm around me at the kitchen sink and asked, "Don't you think you were a little rough on him?"

He had confronted me on behalf of our offended son. I was exposed. The next move was mine. After a period of reflection and cooling off, I gained the courage to apologize to Tim.

"It's OK, Mom," he said in his deepening voice. Then he confronted me with a wise observation of painful truth: "You're not perfect. This is just one of those things you haven't learned to handle yet."

Experiences in this sort of open, family honesty have taught me that growing up doesn't happen automatically when we become parents. It takes a lifetime. No matter how long we live, we'll always need to grow. And we will never reach perfect maturity this side of heaven.

In our travels, we picked up a choice slogan about parental maturity: "To be a father is an art; just to become one is not smart." We chuckled when we first read this clever jingle. So simply said!

But how can we be the kind of growing parents who can encourage growth toward the family goal of maturity? The answers have rarely come easily to us. We are finding, though, that they are available.

I thought about this when I heard a minister say that God doesn't make families like kits without instructions. I reflected a bit and realized that He never asks us to do or be anything without supplying every resource we need to carry out His wishes. As He assures us in Philippians 2:13, "It is God who is at work in you, both to will and to work for His good pleasure." How inspirational to recognize that this applies in every area of life, including parenthood with its sticky problems.

Through our parenting years, Walt and I have discovered many helpful, God-given resources. The communities we've lived in have provided schools, churches, medical facilities, community centers, and counseling services, all equipped to meet many of our needs. The nearest library or bookstore also offers a gold mine of helpful information. Surely, no previous generation of parents has had access to so many parenting aids as ours. However, we've also found that we have to approach each of these resources with common sense and spiritually enlightened caution.

Early in my motherhood, I fell into a subtle trap. To help me be the best mother possible, I determined to read every resource book I could find. Most of the books I found, however, set unattainably high standards. They left little room for a slow, natural growing-up process. Their authors had apparently raised their families with great success and no admitted failures.

As I read one book after another, I grew discouraged. For in reality I encountered difficulties the book writers never even hinted at. Further, I met with frustration when I tried many of their guaranteed methods.

This led me to ignore books on parenting. By and large, our family has grown by trial and error under more direct guidance from the Lord. We have sought little assistance from books on "How to raise the perfect family."

Today I detect a more honest and realistic attitude in most current books on family living. But I still hesitate to rely on books to show me how to solve parental dilemmas in "ten easy steps."

As a mother, I have found the two most dependable resources to be the Bible and a direct relationship with God. To begin with, I have claimed God's personal pledge: "All Scripture is . . . profitable for teaching, for reproof, for correction, for training in righteousness; that the man of God may be adequate, equipped for every good work" (2 Timothy 3:16-17). Repeatedly in our experience, the Bible has proved to be just what Paul claimed—an intensely practical guidebook for living. Whenever it hasn't worked for us, the problem has usually been that we have not troubled ourselves to find out what God was really trying to tell us.

Beyond this, we are learning to appropriate an abundance of strength and help through an intimate faith in Christ. For us at least, life is too big, and the challenges of growth too terrifying, to face without this kind of faith. I love the way our *mature* heavenly Father reminds us repeatedly to "trust in the LORD with all your heart, and do not lean on your own understanding. In all your ways acknowledge Him." Then follows the delightful promise: "And He will make your paths straight" (Proverbs 3:5-6).

What is maturity?

After two decades of family growing, we have all changed our concepts of the answer to this question. Martha no longer dons my bedroom slippers and pretends to be a woman. She does talk of someday becoming a wife and a mother. But she knows that is not the final goal. She has caught a glimpse of something beyond all this. She and, it is to be hoped, every member of the family with her are learning

to focus on a broader, more complete goal—maturity as whole persons in Christ. Among other things, this means that we are all recognizing how much we have yet to learn, and how "faithful is He that calleth you, who also will do it" (1 Thessalonians 5:24, KJV).

SUGGESTED READING

Larson, Bruce. *Living on the Growing Edge*. Grand Rapids: Zondervan, 1968.

When life falls into patterns of comfortable tradition, God wants to push us out of our comfort zones into the new and unknown fringes of our lives known as our "growing edges." This is the theme of this little book, which speaks primarily to the subject of church renewal growth. Even so, much of its message is directed to individual and family-relationship problem areas.

3

Hold on to the Excitement

When we were expecting our first baby, Mom Herr gave us a bit of valuable advice. "I hope you'll learn to enjoy your children," she said. "Too many parents never seem to get past the drudgery to the delight. They miss so much."

At first her words seemed easy enough to follow. Our first-born came fashioned to fascinate—little pink toes, dimpled cheeks, winsome smiles. An irresistible person in miniature, she couldn't help but arouse our enthusiasm.

Yet we soon discovered that at times enjoyment and enthusiasm are both unreal and impossible.

One spring morning, I had just finished scrubbing the clothes by hand in what I'm sure must have been the most gigantic bathtub in the world. I turned on the faucet and began the long process of running rinse water. As a precautionary measure, while waiting for the tub to fill, I ran downstairs to check on the activities of my three toddlers.

Bursting through the front door, I found two-year-old Tim digging with a stick in the garden. Beside him on the cobblestone walk lay three of his daddy's prize tulips, stems badly mangled and petals drooping. I ignored his not-too-innocent grin and hasty "Lookie, Mommy," and went through the scolding-spanking routine which had been well-established in recent weeks since the tulips began to bloom Then I picked up the wailing young truant and carried him to the kitchen to clean him up.

27

Suddenly I heard running water.

"Oh no!" I gasped.

Then to the boy with muddy hands and teary cheeks, I ordered, "You stay here."

I dashed for the stairs and took all twenty-three steps by two's and three's up to the bathroom. Expecting to be greeted with a rush of cold rinse water, I was only slightly relieved to find the water still sloshing not more than an inch from the top of the tub.

"Thank God," I breathed, as I screwed the big, old faucet tightly. Then I remembered the awful potential for disaster I had left downstairs.

Rushing into the kitchen, I found it empty, so I followed a series of open doors and smudgy footprints to the front yard. There was the baby teetering back and forth on the top step of the porch—ready to plunge to the sidewalk below. Grabbing her, I breathed one more prayer of thanks to God for helping us avert yet another tragedy.

Fifteen years later, I still have those kinds of days. The trash hasn't been emptied, the floor hasn't been vacuumed, the bedrooms resemble the aftermath of a hurricane, and all three teenagers are managing to be impossibly obstinate at the same time. On those days, my shattered enthusiasm for motherhood brings me to the I-want-to-scream-and-run-away point.

But we do have other kinds of days as well. Like the day Tim and I came home late from a doctor's appointment. We had endured a four-hour hurry-up-and-wait round of treatments. Supper should have been served at six o'clock. We hadn't left the clinic until 5:50. I opened the door at home and smelled the delightful aroma of hamburgers. Martha had discovered the buns and meat sitting out to thaw. On her own initiative she had prepared the meal quite expertly and thereby revived my lagging zeal.

Enthusiasm has always come easily for me. But so have

disenchantment and escape strategy. When high school chemistry ceased to be exciting, and the going got rough, I simply went to the dean's office and checked out of the class. I repeated this same routine with college chemistry. All through school, I now realize, I managed to squirm out of things once they lost their appeal.

Something told me, though, that family life had to be different. I came from a broken home. Statistically, this made me a poor risk as a stable marriage partner.

I determined to prove the statistics wrong. Enthusiastic or not, I would stick it out as both wife and mother. There would be no more checking out at the dean's office if I could help it.

Raising three children has surprised me with the revelation that neither marriage nor mothering has to be an endurance test to a bitter finish. Rather, parental enthusiasm can be reasonably sustained and renewed in the pressures of daily family living.

I am finding that the secret lies in recognizing that today in the life of each individual represents only one stage along the road to maturity. A friend who is a successful junior high school teacher says it this way: "I cannot expect the *today* child to be what I think he/she can only become *tomorrow*." This young woman attributes her success in dealing with unstable adolescents to her realization that adolescence is a transitory, unpredictable stage. Adolescence is a tremendously important stage, in every way, but it isn't the end. I believe the same is true of any stage of a child's development—or of our development as adults, for that matter.

Grasping this concept has led me to understand and appreciate these words of Rene Voeltzel: "We must not look too soon in the child for the person he will later become."[1]

I have also found it essential to learn to live in the present with eyes focused on the future.

Occasionally we get down the big box of family snapshots. This always generates a lot of excitement. As each child looks through the envelope containing pictures of himself, I revel in the "oh's" and bashful grins, and answer the "was this really me" questions.

Sometimes I ask, "Would you like to go back and be a baby again? Or be two, or seven, or ten, or twelve again?"

"No way!" Their response is always unanimous. Our temporary, nostalgic journey completed, we return the box to its niche and thank God for continued life to live *today*, reaching toward our *tomorrows*.

These family-album visits with the past remind me of Paul's formula in Philippians 3:13-14 for ongoing living: "But one thing I do: forgetting what lies behind and reaching forward to what lies ahead, I press on toward the goal for the prize of the upward call of God in Christ Jesus."

I was especially charmed by a piece of free verse called "Attics." In the last stanza, the author's imagery captured me as he talked about our need to have a spirit of detachment as we remember the past:

> It is well that we visit our attics,
> but as Mother used to say,
> "Don't drag things down."
> There's beauty and deep meaning in the attic,
> but it mustn't be the living room.
> It's not for changing,
> just remembering,
> And to live is always to change.*
>
> GERHARD FROST

Childhood is, after all, very short. It seems our parent-child-relationship stage passes so quickly into the period of adult interrelationships. Looking back, we see that each

---

*Reprinted from *Bless My Growing* by Gerhard Frost, copyright 1974, by permission of Augsburg Publishing House.

stage along the way has held its own peculiar sweetness as well as its special problems. We are increasingly aware that we pass this way only one time. Don't we owe it to ourselves and our children to enjoy the process that leads us from infancy to the mature persons God planned for us to become?

My maternal grandmother first showed me how to watch for the little things that fascinate and bring enjoyment. Our first child was also a first grandchild and a first great-grandchild on my side of the family. You can imagine the enthusiasm she evoked.

Sometime during those early days of basking in the wonder of four generations, Grandma B. and I were examining this special baby's well-formed features.

"Just think," Grandma said. "One day those little fingers will play with dollies."

When several months later they did indeed hold the first dolly, we all experienced a special thrill. As time went on, we watched Martha develop expertise in handling skill tools with her growing fingers: a toy broom to sweep the floor, a pencil to draw pictures, needle and thread to sew on buttons.

Sixteen years later our whole family attended a high school concert. While the chorus sang, we watched those same "little fingers" caress the piano keys as they elicited magnificent accompaniments. I leaned over and whispered to Grandma, "Remember when she was a baby, and you told me her fingers would one day play with dollies? You didn't tell me the half of it."

My eighty-nine-year-old grandmother smiled and said with a characteristic, mischievous glint in her eye, "Oh, I didn't?"

We laughed and shared a special moment of familial enthusiasm.

Way back when my first urge of excitement over motherhood was beginning to wane, someone said to me, "Count the smiles, the new teeth, the first steps. One day very soon it will all pass and leave you gazing at grown men and women. Capture each phase with your heart and make *today* live!"

Years later, I'm beginning to appreciate the depth of these words. Every time I forget them, one of my teenagers comes up with some new, captivating bit of evidence to remind me that nothing in all the world is half so exciting as growing up in families. The unpredictability of such a life provides the incentive I need to hold on to enthusiasm.

SUGGESTED READING

Tournier, Paul. *The Adventure of Living.* New York: Harper & Row, 1965.

A truly effective book to help you understand, capture, and maintain an excitement for life. "Woe betide those," says Dr. Tournier, "who no longer feel thrilled at anything, who have stopped looking for adventure!" Extremely beneficial for parents looking for meaning in their children's bent for often dangerous escapades (while needing a shove into a few untried areas themselves). Deals with topics such as the meaning of work, taking risks, success and failure, making choices—all from a viewpoint that artfully blends biblical and medical perspectives.

4

Leave a Little Child in the Middle

For several years my mother's migrant missionary work confined her to a dirty, rundown town in central California. Its rough streets and small, cheap, stucco houses made it resemble a shabby, Southwestern movie set—minus the cinematic glamour.

On a weekend visit there, six-year-old Tim startled me with his announcement: "This is a beautiful city!"

I stared out the window through swirling dust clouds to the treeless, gravel yard around my mother's mobile home. I listened to the clanking, crashing, and creaking sounds of a nearby cantaloupe packing shed.

"Beautiful?" I retorted. "This lonely, desolate, dull, little old town? It's so awful I wonder why anybody would ever want to live here."

"But, Mother," my boy protested simply, "Grandma lives here." An expression of impatient wonder in his eyes added, how could you miss anything so obviously marvelous?

I recalled this experience several years later as I read in Gladys Hunt's book, *Honey for a Child's Heart:* "When boys and girls grow bigger and older, they should grow from the outside, leaving a little boy in the middle!"[1]

I recognized here, in poetic language, a repetition of my son's plea to stop ignoring my little girl in the middle. But, what was my little girl like? I had to travel back in time, even beyond the boundaries of clear memory, to find an answer to this one.

I had grown up in the wild woods of southwest Washington. Mother tells me that as a toddler I roamed the woods, made friends of little creatures, picked buttercups, climbed stumps and fallen logs.

When I was three years old we moved into town. New sources of wonder replaced the old: bicycles, elevated sidewalks, steam-engine trains, and ice-cream cones. At this time, too, Mother introduced me to the magical world of books. I still recall tramping up the stairs with her to the tiny library located over the fire station. There we would select a stack of books, then rush home for a visit with our friends, Saggy Baggy Elephant, Little Lost Puppy, Peter Rabbit, and a growing circle of others.

As the years passed, my sense of wonder for life grew increasingly sophisticated. I never quite lost my love for woods and seashores and creatures, however. In fact, during a brief period in high school, I turned into a serious collector of a variety of nature specimens. But little by little other things grew more important to me—things like career planning, marriage, and the building of a home.

In my eagerness to grow up, I naively lumped the characteristics of childhood into one category and called them *childish*. Selfishness, rudeness, impulsiveness, foolishness—these belonged to "children." Now that I had become a woman, I wanted to be done with my immature past. It never occurred to me that such virtues as tender emotions, a sense of wonder, lighthearted playfulness, uncomplicated faith, and enjoyment of simple pleasures also belonged to childhood.

Then I became a mother. At the moment the nurse put my first baby into my arms, I experienced childlike wonder that I had never dreamed possible. I was convinced that all of life would be forever dull next to this climactic experience.

Instead, I watched amazed as the mundanenesses of life

took on fresh wonder. I began to see the whole world through the eyes of a baby. I even suspected that my renewed enjoyment of bumblebees and buttercups was somehow childlike.

But in my zeal for parental excellence, I soon pushed the glory aside to ignore once more the voice of my little girl in the middle. I had to concentrate on practical, unglamorous concerns like picking up toys, scrubbing perpetually dirty faces, and keeping curious little hands out of the bookcase. I became so conscious of duty that I almost lost the wonder of childlike motherhood.

Then the Lord sent Auntie Birdie to our big Dutch house. She was a gifted orphanage worker from Ireland. As she spent the summer with us, she gave me the courage and some basic know-how to relax and interact with my children at the childlike level.

One afternoon we were watching the three toddlers throw bread to the ducks at our neighborhood pond. Tim stooped over to pick up a fallen crumb. Auntie Birdie pointed to the boy's pink, dimpled legs.

"Just look at that perfect little body," she exclaimed. "Don't you marvel at how beautifully your children's bodies are made?"

Marvel at their bodies? I hadn't thought of that in ages. I had been too busy training characters to notice bodies. But now at a friend's urging I did look, and I did marvel at all three attractive embodied personalities. And for several fleeting seconds I actually forgot about my mission to train away childish immaturities.

The experiment felt strange at first. But throughout the summer Auntie Birdie inspired me to try it again and again. She showed me how to take the little ones on my lap and talk with them as if they were real people—to share their imaginary escapades, laugh with them, converse with them on their own level, enter into their childlike world. Under

her guidance, we played games together and used our hands
to create things that had no particular instructional value.
We did it just for the sanctified joy of living, loving, getting
acquainted, and enjoying each other.

Gradually I came to understand with new depth what
Jesus really meant when He said, "Unless you are converted
and become like children, you shall not enter the kingdom
of Heaven" (Matthew 18:3). As I made the effort to follow Auntie Birdie's example, I watched my whole attitude
toward life and motherhood grow increasingly childlike.

During the next decade, my growing young family led me
down dozens of delightful paths of childlikeness. The children coaxed me to enter into their spirit of lighthearted
playfulness, which turned many a family outing into a treasured memory. They urged me to share their wonder over
a fruit jar full of June bugs, a mud-spattered truck that
"looks like cinnamon toast," a pond covered with "frog
leaves." They taught me to laugh at myself, even when I
burn the beans or get lost trying to find the discount Levi
store.

Then, just when they had fully stimulated me and
brought me to a point of unparalleled enjoyment of life's
beauty and the wonders of childlike perception, they began
to belittle the whole idea themselves. One Mother's Day,
as we prepared to go on our annual outing to a nearby rose
garden, they groaned and told me it was a "dumb, boring
idea." Later, Martha avoided a family camping trip by
spending the month with relatives. Tim began hiding under the covers when I tried to kiss him good night. They
all expressed a growing distaste for science classes, scenic TV
specials, and classical music.

I was shattered.

"Don't fret, Mama," Walt consoled me. "They're perfectly normal. I suspect you were like this once yourself."

A few moments of honest reflection played back some

strikingly similar scenes from my own sophisticated stage. I remembered the days when I too had sought to escape childhood by discarding childlikeness. I had to admit that my husband was right.

Then together, while the children concentrated on developing their independent adult personalities, we set about to invent subtle ways to help our growing brood preserve each one's little child in the middle.

What an adventure! We soon found, by trial and error, that we could accomplish our goal most effectively by continuing to let our own little child perform for the whole family to see. Which means, when my son refuses to let me kiss him, I occasionally chase him around the house until I corner him and steal a hasty, puckered pass at the hand with which he shields his face. When I sing to the kids to awaken them in the morning, they always beg me to stop torturing them. So I've learned to show mock pain as I scold them for being so inconsiderate of my rare talent display. Usually stalking off in an obviously affected huff, I leave them shaking their heads and muttering, "What a weird mother!"

Our plan seems to be working. We are noticing that their inner, childlike cores are surviving well. Our children have an abundance of silly moments, playful episodes, journeys into imaginative adventure. They bring their friends home and exchange stories about "our goofy parents." And something in the way they groan at our sick jokes tells us that if we ever quit sharing these gems of atrocious humor, they will begin to worry about us.

Nor have they ceased to inspire our own childlike expressions. As parents of teenagers, we experience many days when our hectic world of decisions and responsibilities threatens to destroy the vital seed of our inner child. But always at these desperate points, our children enter the scene as divinely appointed guardians of the fragile seed. With their youthful laughter, dreams, and insight they water, warm, and nourish this seed into constant renewal. I am impressed that at each new growing season of our lives, the tender plants bloom with a richer, more fragrant spray of blossoms.

On the other hand, we sometimes still feel a twinge of pain when Tim insists he hates biology, when nobody wants to take a sightseeing trip to the beach, or when my best efforts at flower arranging draw scarcely more than a prodded grunt or a reluctant "Yeah, it's OK, I guess."

Often as I remind myself how it was with me, I thank God that He planned for childlikeness to be preserved in cycles. Then hope revives that someday, when Martha, Tim, and Mary Jane have become parents, one more generation will take over the education process and arouse their little children in the middle to full consciousness.

I suspect that when this happens the wonder will increase for us all—for them, because they will possess a deeper maturity to help them interpret and appreciate life's childlike pleasures, and for us, because we will enter the extra special growth stage of grandparenthood. Yes, even for God Himself, whose love for our children is accompanied by the limitless power to perfect His work of art in each of them.

All our lives we have drawn encouragement and assurance from God's promise: "My word . . . shall not return unto me void, but it shall accomplish that which I please, and it shall prosper in the thing whereto I sent it" (Isaiah 55:11, KJV). We have always applied this to matters of spiritual development. Today we have begun to claim it for our children and ourselves as whole persons—bodies, spirits, intellects, emotions, all growing up around our little child in the middle.

5

Life Isn't Fair

For a long time, Walt and I believed that Air Force kids were especially gifted at adjusting to new places and people. At least they got plenty of practice as they were shuttled around the world like perpetual tourists. Besides, we worked with a lot of them in chapel programs, and they seemed normal enough to us.

Our own children devastated our lovely, hopeful theory, however. Once they started school, they convinced us that mobility does not always develop adaptability. For them it had the opposite effect. Each move produced near traumas, until we saw a pattern of deepening insecurities emerge.

Being the oldest, Martha suffered the most. In November of her fourth grade year, we made our last military move. She had encountered increasing difficulty making friends ever since she had entered school, six moves back. But this latest relocation threatened to destroy what little relating ability she had managed to retain.

She came home from school in tears that first afternoon.

"Mommy, take me back to the school we just came from," she sobbed.

"What's the matter with this one?" I queried, recalling other similar first-day experiences.

"Nobody likes me!"

"What happened?" I coaxed my trembling daughter to my side on the couch.

"They laughed at me and called me names. Nobody would play with me. They all hate me!"

She buried her head in my lap. I stroked her auburn hair. Somehow I must find a way to smooth out the bumps, to even the score, to make life fair for her.

"Take it easy, dear," I soothed. "Tomorrow will be better. Remember? It always works that way."

But tomorrow turned out to be worse. So did all the tomorrows in that place. I did everything I could to balance the scales of justice during that long winter. I offered some words of sage advice, collected over the years:

"Be a friend; then surely someone will respond." (*No one did.*)

"We'll only be here till June." (*To a child that hurts, June is like the end of time.*)

"Sticks and stones. . . ." (*This one simply isn't so, and we finally had to admit it.*)

I tried to make home as pleasant as I could. Even here I met insurmountable barriers. Walt worked graveyard shift and had to have the house quiet in order to sleep in the daytime. Nor could the children play outside, for we were receiving a record rainfall that year. As a result, home often became one more pressure point, when it should have served as a welcome relief from pressure.

Finally, in desperation, I visited Martha's schoolteacher, a tired-looking young woman behind a cluttered desk.

"Your daughter's living through a nightmare," she told me. "I've tried all the tricks I know to help her. Every one seems to make the situation worse."

"But why?" I asked. "What is she doing wrong?"

"Nothing more than any constantly rejected child would naturally do. She tries so hard. Maybe too hard—I don't know. Apparently she's a victim of the standard treatment for all newcomers in this place. It's called 'kill by neglect.' "

Then, hanging her head, she concluded with visible difficulty. "I feel it with her, Mrs. Herr. I'm new too. And it's my first year of teaching."

In June, our Air Force days over, we moved again—this time to a new life in a new place. We hoped Martha would find some success in her social relationships. But while the new community proved to be more congenial, the trauma of her latest experience had sharpened the girl's sensitivity and made her painfully reluctant to expose herself to the threat of further rejection.

To this day, making and keeping friends is difficult for her. This is not entirely bad, however. Martha's encounter with rejection is helping her develop the art of handling social problems. She's also gaining a tender touch with others who need acceptance. And she can appreciate the deep values of both family and committed friendships.

"Growing up is, among other things, accepting the fact that nothing in this life is ever perfect," writes Eileen Guder in *God, but I'm Bored.*[1] I like this. However, I'm convinced that acceptance is only the beginning. For whenever I do no more than give assent to the less-than-satisfying truth that life is imperfect, even unfair, I find myself growing pessimistic, bitter, and cynical. The trick, I'm learning, is to change a negative fact into a positive force for good.

Early in life I encountered the need for this ability. Until I turned ten years old, my father and I were inseparable companions. We shared motorcycle rides, picnics, outings to a railroad roundhouse, and a million and one other togethernesses.

This all came to an abrupt end when my parents were separated by divorce. Our broken home shattered my world. Those were the days when divorce, especially among Christians, was still considered a disgrace. I had heard both of my parents speak out against it, and I certainly never expected them to resort to it. I could not understand, nor could I even accept the truth for a long while.

One thing seemed clear to me: my daddy had forsaken me. For months, I grieved over the loss—almost as if he had died. When he came to visit us on one occasion, I shut myself away in my room with my memories and tears and refused to see him.

As the months turned into years, the deeper levels of love for my father eventually healed the wounds. Once more we developed a friendship that lasted well and survived other severe tests.

From this early encounter with pain, I began to learn that grief can be a healthy part of growth. Without it, emotional injury would fester like a tightly closed puncture wound, where blood cannot flow and infection sets in. As free-flowing blood cleanses a physical wound, so the natural expression of grief helps to heal injured relationships.

My parents' reaction to the breakup of their marriage taught me another important lesson in facing and using life's adversities for positive ends. Throughout the years since their divorce, I have never heard either parent speak critically of the other. Instead, I have watched them build new, productive lives for themselves and go on growing. And I have decided that no matter how we suffer from each other's mistakes, we can grow stronger if we refuse to allow bitterness and hatred to enter our lives.

As our children have grown, we have tried consistently to be fair with them. But we have found this isn't always possible or even desirable. Together we have been uncovering a lot of evidence that while life isn't fair, it is tremendously worth living.

I particularly remember a discovery we made on a summer morning family hike through the California redwoods. At one point we had to walk wide to the left of the path to avoid a large madrone tree that jutted out from a steep embankment. It bent almost horizontally over the path. Then it turned sharply upward and grew straight and tall.

"What a tremendous feat of natural architecture!" I observed.

"Imagine the tons of snow and driving wind and rain it supports each winter," Walt added.

Then I remembered that, the previous winter, thousands of similar trees in the mountains near our home had snapped under an unusually heavy load of ice and snow. "Too brittle to take it," the newspapers had reported. They lacked the elasticity to resist extreme pressures.

What made the difference between those trees and this odd-shaped madrone before us in the pathway? Perhaps life had treated the brittle trees a bit more fairly. Considering the difference in climate of the two locations, I suspected they had seen fewer severe storms. I also noted that the madrone tree had apparently had an early meeting with tragedy. A landslide had toppled and nearly uprooted it while it was probably still a sapling.

Living together as a family has brought us some untimely landslides and shattered dreams. Undoubtedly we will face more of these unhappy experiences in the future. We hope we can accept each difficult event as a challenging avenue for personal and family growth. At least we now know that the secret lies in availing ourselves of the spiritual resources God offers us and in perfecting the art of daily bending and bearing in a world that is never truly fair.

We have also gained a clearer understanding of God as our wise and loving Father. Martha's encounter with painful rejection, that last winter we were with the Air Force, opened our eyes to this.

At each fresh twist of the knife in our daughter's heart, we felt a deepening, vicarious pain. Even worse, we experienced a helpless frustration quite strange to us as parents.

Our child was hurting. Yet we could do little, if anything, to alleviate her suffering.

Yes, we did talk about taking her "back to the school we just came from." It was only a hundred miles away. We had just spent eighteen months there in our hometown, while Walt served an isolated duty tour in Thailand. With Daddy coming home on weekends, we could make do. After all, even weekends together would be better than living half a world apart as we had just done. We didn't entertain the possibility for long, however. Something told us that this was no answer; running away from problems solves nothing and usually adds new frustrations to an already complex situation.

That winter, as we searched the Scriptures for some consolation and some answers, we saw fresh pictures of the perfect Father interacting with His children. And in the years since, I have gone on studying the subject.

I have watched God evict Adam and Eve from the Garden of Eden to live with the consequences of rebellion. Surely, He could have patched things up and made do—maybe by giving them another chance. Such a move might have looked more just. Instead He punished them, because judgment was the only way to lasting justice. I'm sure, though, that He did it with an aching heart.

I have listened to Paul pleading with God to deliver him from the thorn in his flesh. This tender Father said (again with tears in His voice, I'm sure), "My grace is sufficient for you. You need My grace, My strength, rather than deliverance from the pain that will make you strong" (2 Corinthians 12:9, author's paraphrase).

In Isaiah 30:18, I found these words: "Therefore the Lord longs to be gracious unto you, and therefore He waits on high to have compassion on you. For the LORD is *a God of justice;* how blessed are all those who long for Him" (italics added).

During the difficult months at the end of Walt's military career, our family faced many apparent injustices. We came out of the experience with a new appreciation for the God who has committed Himself to our welfare, even when it involves allowing us to hurt. With renewed adoration, we saw Him too as the Father who has promised us there is a day coming when "He shall wipe away every tear" from our eyes (Revelation 21:4), and when life will at last be truly fair.

6

Ask Me No Questions

Nine-year-old Tim crawled into bed one night a bit more quietly than usual. When I leaned over to kiss him good night, I detected an uneasy solemnity not normal in active, third grade boys. I knew he had had some rough times in school lately. His teacher had told me that he seemed constantly preoccupied.

So I perched myself on the edge of his bed. Perhaps tonight I could get to the bottom of the problem. Cautiously I probed, trying to persuade him to talk about his troubles. Surely, no third grader could have worries so great that his mother could not be of some assistance, I reasoned.

But when he finally shared his questions, I discovered I was unprepared.

"How can I be sure all you've told me about God is true?" he blurted out. "None of my friends at school believe the way you do."

I stared at my young son in perplexed silence. Where could I find an answer that would satisfy him? More important, how should I handle the panicky feeling in my own heart? Was all my teaching in vain?

I thought back to the innocent and amusing kinds of questions he had asked when he was a very little guy. Like that other night, five years earlier, when he had looked up at the sky and pointed with his finger.

"Daddy, can you pick me a star?" he asked. "I want that big one over there."

"No, son," his daddy had replied, "I can't quite reach it."

"Why not?"

"Because God set it up too high."

"No, He didn't, Daddy." Tim was always persistent when he wanted a thing. "Just get the ladder and climb it right up there and get me the star."

I also pictured him sitting on the floor, endlessly taking apart his toys, trying to put them back together, and then capitulating with, "Daddy, please fix." It seemed to me now, sitting beside my confused third grader, that all his life he had been asking things, trying to discover how things were put together, searching for answers in one way or another.

Often all three of the youngsters had driven me to distraction with their incessant questions. At times I found it easy to turn off my ears and simply nod assent. Or to try to hush them with, "You ask too many questions," or "Can't you see I'm busy?" I had to admit that it was sometimes simpler this way than stopping to give them full attention and honest answers.

I had never questioned their right to ask, however. In fact, over the years of living with my family, I had decided that inquisitiveness was a healthy sign of growing minds. How could children learn if they didn't show enough curiosity to look for information and practical skills?

My little ones had taught me that no matter how trivial or how ridiculous it may seem to me, a question deserves to be regarded with the same seriousness that prompts a child to ask it. I began to learn that a warm, positive response constitutes an invitation to "ask me another."

The times I felt best about were those when I had not been too quick to dispense my knowledge. Instead, we had gone to the library for just the right book or taken a walk in the garden to share in the discovery of an answer.

I found that by carefully chosen questions and guided observations, interspersed with a few gems of knowledge to fill in the gaps, I could stimulate a curious child to even greater curiosity levels. I believed that a part of my parental function was not primarily to dispense information but to stretch young minds. The world is already full of people who have never learned to think for themselves. I determined not to add to the problem. Yes, one of my greatest gifts to my children (and through them to the world) would be to help them begin to develop the art of thinking and asking questions.

But tonight, at my son's bedside, I sensed that I was facing a new kind of problem. His latest questions had nothing to do with information. These were deep questions—the kind that strike at the foundation of essential relationships to each other, to ourselves, and to God. Up to this point I had been confident of the formula: Strong training + strong example = strong Christian offspring.

Somewhat blinded by idealism (and perhaps a tinge of cowardice), I had never considered seriously the possibility that before my children's faith could be truly their own, it must first pass the test of scrutiny by deep questioning—maybe even occasional doubting.

I had forgotten some of the elements of the pattern of my own youth. Now I remembered a time when I too had questioned the basic tenets of my faith. Yet fear had held me back from pursuing, exposing, or even admitting my questions and doubts. Consequently they had followed me far into adulthood, until I finally faced and reckoned with them.

Was this what I wanted for my son? Could I help him dismiss all the fears and doubts with a prepackaged set of theologically correct, pat answers? I was tempted to try. But, no, I didn't dare.

"Son," I began slowly, praying each word into expression,

"I've always told you that most people you meet won't believe in Jesus. This doesn't mean He's not real."

"But how can I know for sure?" he pleaded.

"You have to start by asking God Himself. Tell Him all about your doubts, your questions, your friends. Ask Him to show you what is right."

"How will I know when He's showing me?"

"I don't know how He'll do it. With each of us He works differently." *Was I really saying all this?* "But you'll know, son. You'll know."

Our discussion proved to be a turning point in both our lives. Just when he got his answers, I don't know. Perhaps he doesn't know himself. For that matter, he is still asking—and still receiving answers. I have learned, too, that I must admit the limits of my knowledge and even ask questions of my own.

Several years after Tim's experience with doubts, I faced the problem with one of our daughters. Always eager to share her feelings with me, Martha went through a spell, in her early teens, when she kept mostly to herself. Then one night she asked if we could talk. She began with small talk about school, wardrobes, friends. Little by little she changed the direction and cracked open the door to her inner self. Finally, she said with a tone of urgency in her voice, "Mom, I've got to ask you something. It's important."

"Ask on," I invited.

"I'm afraid you'll be upset with me."

"Try me."

Haltingly she ventured, "How do I know there is a God?" Then she relaxed and let the words gush out: "Does He really love me? Did He really save me? What good does it do to be a Christian when all my friends are having such fun being sinners?"

Once more I felt that twinge of painful inadequacy for the questions of the moment. But I recalled a previous encounter with a child's doubts and reminded myself that even parental concern need not make me panic.

"I didn't want to tell you," she confided, "because I didn't want to hurt your feelings or disappoint you."

"Disappoint me? Never!" I managed this one with something akin to assurance. "I asked those same questions when I was your age. It frightened me, too. But I never found a real faith, all my own, until I struggled with the deep issues and got hold of God's answers for myself."

"Ask me no questions, I'll tell you no lies," goes the well-known saying. Experience in mothering and in reading the Bible have convinced me the proverb should read like this: *Ask me no questions, and I'll question whether you are growing.*

I was fascinated to realize that the great men in Scripture all asked questions of God—not just little surface questions, either.

When Moses' mission to Egypt appeared to be doomed, he demanded, "Why did You send me here?" (Exodus 5: 22, author's paraphrase).

Job cried out in agony from an ash heap, "Why was I born to suffer?" (Job 3:20, author's paraphrase).

"How long will You forget me, O Lord?" asked David, the man after God's own heart (Psalm 13:1, author's paraphrase).

Thomas presented an ultimatum of doubt: "Unless I shall see in His hands the imprint of the nails . . . I will not believe" (John 20:25).

Peter, always impetuously sure of himself, but never quite ready to trust God, actually rebuked Jesus with the question, "How can this be?" (Matthew 16:22, author's paraphrase).

In my biblical studies of God-man relationships, I have been thrilled to learn that God never reprimanded anyone for asking a sincere question. Rather, to every intense seeker after truth and mercy, He gave not only answers but a place close to His heart.

I am truly grateful that Jesus Himself urged His followers, "Ask, and it shall be given you; seek, and ye shall find; knock, and it shall be opened unto you" (Matthew 7:7, KJV).

And, thanks to a son and two daughters who have dared to air their doubts, I have concluded that we must banish complacency with the question mark if we would know anything real about growth and contentment.

SUGGESTED READING

Howe, Reuel. *The Creative Years*. Greenwich, Conn.: Seabury, 1959.

A particularly helpful book for parents in their mid-thirties and forties. Much attention is given to needs of adolescents, parents, and marriage partners in this difficult period of life. Articulate, well illustrated by anecdotes, keen observations, and clear statements of workable life principles.

7

Let Go and Let Grow

In her sophomore year in high school, Martha asked me, "Why do you and Dad trust us kids so much? You wouldn't believe the restrictions most of our friends live with. Their parents don't trust them at all!"

Why indeed? If only I could pull back the curtain of her memory a few short years to the summer she was thirteen. But probably she wouldn't remember the incident that remains so vivid in my mind.

She had just returned from church camp on a hot summer afternoon. Recalling glowing stories I had heard of spiritual transformations out under the redwoods and stars, I expected a new thirteen-year-old to come home and astonish us with her renovated disposition. And some real renovating would have been welcome at that period of her development.

Our oldest had never posed any big problems. But she did exert a strong will. When she reached adolescence, the ways she chose to assert her independence and vent her personal frustrations kept me constantly on edge. Realistically, I had expected the teen years to involve difficult adjustments. Nonetheless, her daddy and I both believed strongly in the doctrine of parental determinism. Our children's growth rested in our hands as parents. Hence, we must maintain firm control. So, at her every rebellious outbreak we clamped down harder. She fought back.

I don't recall the things we tangled about. Probably they were mostly routine issues, like messy beds, dishes, and curfews.

With maddening composure, Walt reminded me again and again, "Take it easy, Mama. She'll grow up someday."

Impatient to see his words prove prophetic—but *now*—I was keenly disappointed when she returned home from camp unimproved. In fact, she was even crankier than before she had left. Once more our wills clashed, igniting the inter-generation sparks. In no time the angry girl had stormed off to her bedroom. The door banged behind.

Unnerved, I retreated to *my* bedroom and tried to pray. "O Lord," I began. I couldn't go on. I had prayed the rest so often in recent weeks and had received never a hint to an answer. So I lay across my bed and sobbed.

Suddenly the words of a familiar Scripture verse marched into my consciousness: "Let not your heart be troubled." I sensed that God was speaking directly to me. "Ye believe in God, believe also in me" (John 14:1, KJV).

With fatherly gentleness, the Lord seemed to be telling me, "Dear, harried child, relax. All these years you've taught and fretted over this girl. Now, it's My turn. Remember, I've been your teacher for a long time. Can you trust Me to teach your daughter as well?"

What a challenge! Lying there on my bed, listening to the heavenly voice in my heart, I thought it all seemed so reasonable. With fresh vision and excitement, I yielded to the suggestion.

I soon found, though, that learning to trust the Lord beyond the limits of parental determinism meant learning to be a parent all over again. I began to agree with Reuel Howe, who said in a practical book for parents of adolescents, "The habit of paternalism is hard for us to break."[1]

This kind of confidence involved trusting the children as well. Trusting teenagers seemed like a risky idea to both

Walt and me. We were sharply aware that we could alter the course of a whole life by a single decision to grant freedom to an immature child.

Further, we weren't used to this sort of parenting. During the early, formative years, when they were still willing to be called children, we had placed a multitude of restrictions on our little ones. We insisted on knowing where they were, who they were with, and what they were doing twenty-four hours a day. We saturated their minds and schedules with value teaching, Bible training, cultural activities. They needed these things to help them lay a solid foundation on which to build their own independent adult lives someday.

As we analyzed the situation, we realized that as they had shown evidence of maturity, we had already begun to relax some of the restrictions and let them bear an increasing share of the responsibility for their own decisions. Now, just when they were reverting to childish ways we thought they had outgrown, we sensed a need to let go and let God take over.

Making this realization practical has not been a simple matter. At times, we still wonder when to trust and when to hold the reins of authority a little longer. But we are learning to seek guidance from the Father who asks us to trust Him, to act as we believe best, and then to leave the outcome with Him.

One of our first experiences with this principle involved music lessons. When both of our girls met the piano, it was instant fascination. We started Martha's lessons in the third grade. She progressed with commendable speed and no lack of enthusiasm. In her junior high years, however, her attitude began to change. She resented her lessons. Coercion seemed increasingly necessary, yet proved to be decreasingly satisfactory.

At last, we had to face the ultimate question: Should we

let her drop the lessons? We weighed the alternative sides of the issue. She might never return to the piano. What a loss! On the other hand, would our insistence kill her interest? Or, worse yet, would it endanger an all-important personal relationship with our teenager?

For two years, we struggled with the decision. After her junior high graduation, we stopped the lessons and gave her eager, little sister a turn. We waited to see how the story would end.

At first, "Mary Had a Little Lamb" and simple one-octave scales replaced the Debussy and Bach we had been accustomed to. But this didn't last long. Our daughter who had fought against lessons could not resist the lure of the keyboard. Back she went to her beloved piano. Now, without lessons or a prod from her parents, she played hour upon hour. Her improvement astounded us all.

Today, our budget can't keep pace with Martha's hunger for new music. At school and church her services are in constant demand. She is thanking us for letting her find her own way to musical and personal growth. Mary Jane is rapidly taking her place alongside her sister as an accomplished pianist. We have concluded that, after all, this was one of those times when it was best to let go and let grow.

And what if the story had turned out differently? What if Martha had never returned to her music? Would this have proved that our confidence was misplaced? This question disturbed us for awhile. Then the Lord reminded me, "My thoughts are not your thoughts, neither are your ways my ways, saith the LORD. For as the heavens are higher than the earth, so are my ways higher than your ways" (Isaiah 55:8-9, KJV).

Through this experience we decided that indeed the Lord is able to apply whatever pressure and guidance are necessary to perfect His plans in our children's lives. We shuddered to realize how much we could have hindered

His work had we continued to apply parental discipline and thereby strain parent-child communication to the breaking point.

Many times I have asked myself what I would do if one of our children married unwisely, if a daughter became pregnant out of wedlock, if our son joined the drug culture, if any one or all three rebelled against Christ. Could I handle these kinds of catastrophes? Would I be able then to bravely affirm with the writer whom I read recently that "actually the more serious danger is not that the adolescents will make mistakes or disgrace themselves and their parents, but that they will not . . . grow up"[2]?

I honestly cannot say how I would react. I hope I'll never have to find out. But I have no assurance of this. The Lord could call on Walt and me to join the thousands of Christian parents who have had to face such disappointments. I have known a few parents who allowed strong personal hurts to hinder forgiveness and acceptance. I have watched many more come through with parental love intact and warm.

Which kind of parent would I be? Until such a time, I can only pray that should the situation arise, I will be able to draw strength from the psalmist's words, "I would have despaired unless I had believed that I would see the goodness of the LORD in the land of the living. Wait for the LORD; be strong, and let your heart take courage; yes, wait for the LORD" (Psalm 27:13-14) .

In the meantime, the Lord has let us face a few relatively minor disappointments. There was the high school spring musical that Walt and I disapproved. At first we planned to forbid our two high schoolers to participate. Then we reconsidered.

"Maybe the play's not as bad as we think," we reasoned. We read the script, and decided we could never support such a production. We discussed our feelings with the children, listened to their reactions, then prayed that the Lord would lead them to see it as we did.

Both teenagers tried out for the play and got parts. We began to ask ourselves where we had gone wrong in training them for good judgment.

"I think we'd better step in now and put an end to this," Walt said one night.

But when we approached the subject, Martha and Tim assured us that they had prayed about their involvement. Before God they felt right about it. Once more we heard God's voice saying, "Can you trust Me with your son and daughter?"

Anxiously we waited for Him to change their minds. He didn't. On performance night, we honored our commitment and stayed home. We smarted with the pains of failure, while our son made his stage debut and Martha did an outstanding piece of piano accompaniment. We were told they would have made any parent proud.

When the cheering died down and our young people emerged, they had a personal message for their perplexed parents. "Thank you, Mom and Dad," they said, "for letting us make our own decision about this play. We understand the way you feel. In fact, we admit that just maybe you were right. But we're so glad you didn't force us to live by your convictions. We think we have the greatest parents in the world."

Why do we trust our kids so much? Certainly not because we are so wise or so full of faith in God. We give the credit to our heavenly Father. Through constant interaction with our children, we have felt Him liberate us from a lot of needless fretting. For He has been showing us that a successful home is not one where everything is always done right. Rather, it is the place where we can help each other succeed or allow each other to disagree, even to fail. Yet always we go on loving, accepting, growing. A successful

Christian home, we have decided, is one where we trust one another by ultimately trusting the Lord our God.

SUGGESTED READING

Bowman, Mary D. *Mom, You Gotta Be Kiddin'*. Old Tappan, N.J.: Revell, 1968.

Here is a fascinating collection of one mother's reactions to her teenagers' growth into responsible adulthood. Mrs. Bowman reveals her struggles to practice self-confidence during the hours of "darkest adolescence." Light, humorous approach with penetrating observations. If you have teenagers, you'll identify. Your teenagers may enjoy it as well. Mine do!

Dobson, James. *Hide or Seek*. Old Tappan, N.J.: Revell, 1974.

This excellent book deals with the topic of self-esteem and why and how to help our children like themselves. A must for every parent in today's negative society.

Part 2

SHARING DISCOVERIES: AN EXPERIENCE OF WONDER

Mary Jane has two loves. The first is cats—kittens, tigers, leopards, lions—all kinds and sizes of cats. She papers her walls with their pictures, collects lion puppets, and grieves inconsolably when a live pussy pet dies or disappears.

Her second love is allegorical fantasies. Long ago Grandma Alice gave us a children's version of *Pilgrim's Progress*. Long before she learned to read, Mary Jane adopted it as her own personal literary prize. I read it to her so many times I nearly memorized it.

Then, when I thought I couldn't take one more line of Little Pilgrim, we found C. S. Lewis's *Chronicles of Narnia*—seven fascinating volumes of allegorical fantasy having a lion as the main character. Here was a guaranteed winning combination for Mary Jane.

In these new pages we met Aslan, the Great Lion, who represents Jesus Christ. In the first book, He sacrifices his life and is resurrected for the redemption of the imaginary world, Narnia, from the curse of the White Witch. Throughout the series Aslan protects, appears to, talks with, and disciplines those who believe in Him and love Him.

For weeks we shared the masterfully told adventures of Aslan and His friends and foes. Then, on a rare summer evening of alone-to-getherness, we shared the last few chapters of the final volume.

With misting eyes and mounting emotion, I read aloud Mr. Lewis's imaginative account of God's last judgment and the opening of heaven's gates to His children. This was not our first imaginary journey into heavenly splendor. Many times, we had accompanied Little Christian into the Celestial City of *Pilgrim's Progress.*

But tonight was special. Lewis and his Aslan had prepared us for a big difference. A sense of wonder and adoration for the God who could plan such glories and bring us all to Himself overwhelmed us both. We talked long that night about how beautiful the real heaven will be. We thought of the many happy reunions we will enjoy there with friends from all around the world. We rejoiced at the idea of meeting our favorite Bible characters. We exulted over the tantalizing prospects of being near Jesus Christ.

Then, with a sudden sparkle in her blue, blue eyes, Mary Jane wrapped up her enthusiasm in the girlish terms that best expressed her inner depths, "Someday, Mommy, when Jesus comes again, I'll rub my face in a lion's mane and hug and kiss it!"

"Dear Lord," I prayed, "what an exquisite, childlike expression of my daughter's personal involvement with You! Thank You for using an allegory and a cat to meet her where she is and prepare her heart for future, maturing levels of worshipful devotion."

This was only one of many treasured discoveries our children have shared with us. In our family, we are finding that life is an adventurous series of discoveries—discovering persons, learning ideas and skills, experiencing moments of wonder.

Paul wrote in Philippians 4:8: "Whatever is true, whatever wins respect, whatever is just, whatever is pure, whatever is lovely, whatever is of good repute, if there is any virtue, or anything deemed worthy of praise—cherish the thought of these things" (Weymouth*).

Part 1 of this book dealt with the attitudes necessary for growth. Part 2 considers how, by the cherishing of these things, chosen from among the daily doings of family life, we can go on from loving life to sharing discoveries, for a richer, more exciting growth *together.*

---

*Richard Francis Weymouth, *The New Testament in Modern Speech.*

8

Self Is Not a Naughty Word

One night at an open house, Mary Jane's fifth grade teacher approached me. "I'd like to know what goes on at your house," the young bachelor said. "All three of your children are unusually creative. What do you do to them?"

Dumbfounded, I mumbled, "I don't know. I never gave it a thought."

"There has to be a reason," he prodded.

I began hesitantly, "We didn't own a TV until about three years ago. The kids had to find other ways to entertain themselves."

Groping for other clues, I went on, "We also bought them very few toys. When they wanted something, they usually discovered a way to make it. We tried to provide them with plenty of materials to work with. And we also praised their efforts, no matter how crude the results. Beyond this, I've no idea."

The man smiled and smoothed out his dark moustache. "Whatever you did, you surely did it right," he concluded.

I went home reviewing the past decade and a half of parenting as I searched for a basic answer to Mr. Fifth Grade Teacher's question—one that would satisfy my own mind. For weeks I mulled it over. I had to sort through dozens of memorable scenes until I found the key.

I recalled four-year-old Tim, sitting on the floor and surrounded by newspapers, string, sticks, scissors, and a bottle of glue. All day long he sat there, cutting, pasting, tearing apart, and starting over, determined to make a kite "like Mikie's."

I heard Martha picking out simple tunes on the old, rented, Dutch piano.

I remembered Mary Jane's first garment sewed for her favorite doll. It was hardly a winning entry for a fashion show. Yet each hand-stitch was a triumphant step on the road to self-discovery as a seamstress.

Suddenly I caught myself using the word "self-discovery." Could that be the key? Was that what was going on at our house? At first, I wasn't too sure I liked the implications of the idea. After all, self was something to avoid, certainly not to discover or develop.

All our lives, Walt and I had been taught to fear the word *self*. Hadn't Jesus told us, "If any man will come after me, let him deny himself" (Luke 9:23, KJV)? Wasn't *self* that petty, egocentric, selfish part of our character that made us less than likable before God and others?

Yet, now that I brought the idea out and examined it, I suspected that *self* might have another definition. Maybe it was not always a naughty word. I wondered, could *self* also refer to our inner persons and have all sorts of potential for good? Perhaps this emerging *self* was the real *me* that God considers to be worth the ultimate investment of His love and patience.

Without our realizing it, our narrow view of self had been challenged and broadened by parenthood. I chuckled now to recall a previous encounter with this self in our first toddler, years ago.

Two-year-old Martha had been misbehaving all day. Then, just when her daddy and I had about reached the end of our patience, she suddenly became sweet and cooperative. Busying herself with a fresh round of innocent activities, she began to sing: "Jesus loves me, dis I know."

In an adjacent room, Walt and I exchanged exasperated grins, as the child went on singing. When she came to the phrase "Jesus loves me when I'm bad," I blurted out to my husband, "How could He?"

Walt snickered. "I wasn't going to say it, but I was thinking the same thing," he confessed.

Though for the moment emotions kept us from seeing the situation clearly, we knew we also loved the young errant. What we didn't fully understand was why we felt this way. Our best explanation was something like, "Parental love is just like that."

Ten years later, in the aftermath of an elementary teacher's startling comments, we got a clearer picture. We realized it was this other creative self that both Jesus and a mischievous toddler's parents could love, even "when I'm bad."

Once over the shock of the realization that *self* could possibly be a respectable word, we went on to uncover new answers to Mr. Fifth Grade Teacher's question. We recognized that raising creative children did not come only from limiting TV and toys while supplying plenty of materials and praise. Stimulating creativity was merely one aspect of a more basic process. We were first of all encouraging the discovery and development of three God-gifted selves.

Today we have come to see that reasonable expectations and generous doses of personal acceptance are equally important building blocks for self-discovery.

A couple of years ago, our high school drama department prepared to produce the musical, *You're a Good Man, Charlie Brown.* Our teenagers gave us several preview readings of the play at home. They had not read far when I stopped them.

"How dreadful!" I exploded. "Why must Lucy be so horribly cruel to Charlie Brown? No wonder he has such a complex."

"Please don't hate Lucy," the kids pleaded with me.

"She's just normal. She and Charlie Brown are both like all of us."

They went on with the reading while I tried to sort out what they had just told me. But I had to stop them once more when Charlie Brown lamented:

> Oh, how could there possibly be
> One small person, as thoroughly, totally, utterly
> Blah as me?*

"Do you mean to tell me you feel like that?" I asked. Wow! Was I a parental failure, if they did!

"Sometimes, yes, Mom," they admitted. "That's why we like Charlie Brown. Laughing and crying with him, and seeing that he really isn't as bad as he thinks he is, makes us feel better about our own not-so-good ideas about ourselves."

The whole idea of self-esteem and family acceptance suddenly looked terribly important to me. I knew that on occasions my children, like Charlie Brown, had experienced the pain of personal rejection by the Lucys in their lives. If, however, they could count on finding acceptance at home, I reasoned, surely they stood a good chance of coming out with strong self-images. In such a warm, family environment, even Charlie Brown could learn to like himself, if the cartoonist would ever let him grow up.

But acceptance must be worked at. We have found one of the best ways to establish it is to spend time with our children and enjoy them. Raymond Rogers said it this way: "The parent who is interested in his child plays with him, works with him, spends time with him, leads him into various kinds of self-activity."[1] I think the key phrase here is "with him."

Sometimes this means simply being there, even if we

---

*Copyright 1965 and 1967, Jeremy Music Inc., used by permission.

don't do a thing. Strolling through the house recently, our fifteen-year-old called, "Mom!"

"Yes?" I shouted from another room. "You need something?"

When he found me, he replied, "No, nothing. Just wanted to know you're here."

Often when Walt is working in the garden or around the house, he'll ask me to join him. "I need you to hold my hand while I work," he'll say with a smile.

I used to picture the absurdity of taking this request literally. I'm beginning now to understand that "Come hold my hand" is a valid, sensible request which really means, "Come share yourself with me."

One summer, as Tim and I cut and pounded away at four rooms and a stairwell full of wallboard, I made one error after another. Finally, in exasperation at my stupidity, Tim counseled me: "Mom, you weren't cut out to be a builder. I think you'd do better to stay with your writing."

Yet, when I suggested that I do just that, he begged me to come back and help. "It's a lot more like fun when you're with me, even if you do do it all wrong," he assured me.

I have thought about this principle often when I have heard or seen the slogan "Everything goes better with Coke." I couldn't resist paraphrasing it with a family twist: Everything goes better with you—a family person who cares enough to share himself in the great self-discovery adventure.

Things also change when we share ourselves. When Tim was in the eighth grade, every afternoon, with religious regularity, he watched the rerun series of a favorite TV comedy. Before long, he had seen each episode at least three times. Still, he would not miss the program.

Then one afternoon, just as the favorite show came on, Walt walked into the room and invited, "Let's go out to the darkroom to print some pictures."

Instantly the boy flicked off the TV and marched off with his father to do a "with me" project. That one incident ended the daily visits with TV reruns. From then on, Tim found more constructive and interesting things to do. Walt's invitation to togetherness had opened for his son a new door to growth at a time when, though Tim was unaware of it, the old pastime was losing its keen hold on him.

In our family, the self-discovery drama has had some unexpected side benefits for us as parents. In the beginning we saw it as a chance to get acquainted with our children, to help them unfold their fascinating potential, to find their beautifully unique selves. We found ourselves applying verses like 1 Thessalonians 5:11: "Therefore, encourage one another, and build up one another, just as you also are doing."

Suddenly we noticed that we too were changing. Many of the old self-images we had cherished so long began to crumble as they were replaced by exciting facets of our ever changing selves we had never dreamed existed.

At times, these special revelations come through our children's unexpected words. One such incident occurred for me the year Walt was in Thailand. I found trying to be both father and mother to three small children an impossible task. I simply couldn't be to them all that I thought duty required.

"Failuritis" was plaguing me one day, when our first grader climbed up on my lap. Draping his chubby arms around my shoulders, he said, "I love you, Mommy. You make the house so nice to live in."

Talk about self-discovery! In that instant my son showed me that my children had never expected me to be a father to them. They had not expected me to be even a temporary one. They were satisfied to take me as I was—a mother. What a relief to know that I had only to be my own self, nothing more.

For the most part, our children, by their daily, winsome ways, have helped us to discard faded self-images and discover our selves.

My generation had espoused some extremely narrow ideas of spirituality and successful Christian life-style. As a result, in my early years of Christian education involvement, I considered arts and crafts more or less a waste of time. In my estimation, only exercises of the spirit counted for anything. I could not understand how working with the hands could communicate God's messages to the heart. When I had tried to do handcrafts as a child, the only message I received from my constant failures was that I was not an artist. In my youthful desire to please God, I could easily dismiss the whole art field as a set of unspiritual trappings.

The arts and crafts our children engaged in as they grew, however, challenged my evaluation. I could not miss seeing the importance of those little crayoned birthday cards, the family Christmas pageant in a stable, the first piano solo, the art pads filled with rough sketches of "pretty girls."

Could it be that the arts were more than art? In my thinking, they emerged gradually as gifts from God—His image expressed in man. They were even helping my children to learn character growth, knowledge, and eternal truth. In fact, they seemed to be providing some essential avenues for spiritual learning, self-discovery, and expression.

This revolutionary, new learning experience paved the way for me eventually to find *myself* as a writer, a creative person, *an artist,* no less!

Today, we think we have found some real answers for that fifth grade teacher. And we are thanking God for what goes on at our house. For as our children keep tugging away at the fringes of our self-awareness, they lead us into fascinating new discoveries about ourselves and confirm our belief that *self* is not a naughty word. They are also teaching us that our mission is not so much to be a blessing as to find and be ourselves and work together in the family to bring each other's self into a wholeness of creative being.

SUGGESTED READING

Tournier, Paul. *The Meaning of Persons.* N.Y.: Harper & Row, 1957.

Written by a noted Swiss physician who is also a vibrant Christian, this book deals with the vital processes of discovering personhood and the value of such discoveries in our lives. You won't skim through this book. Its style is readable but meaty. Many poignant thoughts, beautifully expressed, reward the patient reader. It's a bit heavy reading but well worth the effort if you want a refreshing and deep treatment of the subject.

9

School Is Never Out

The central California farming community where my mother began her missionary work always suffered its hottest days in September. I recall one of those torrid days just before school opened. I was walking home from a friend's house on the other side of town. As my feet scuffed up little clouds of dry dust, my mind worked at a zillion daydreams. Suddenly one amazing thought stopped me in the middle of a dusty step.

"Just think," I said aloud, so as to allow for a full savoring of my startling discovery, "I have only six more years of school left!"

Thereafter, I kept a running countdown of years left to go. I liked school, actually. But the prospect of being free from the compulsion of it tantalized me. I longed for the day when I would be able to make my own choices about education—when, where, what courses, whether or not.

Like most children, I believed all learning took place in classrooms. As I grew and sampled the ever widening variety of experiences life offered me, I began to suspect there was more to learning than this. But it took several years of motherhood to reveal the extent of this truth to me.

We watched all three of our little ones learn rapidly during their preschool years. Convinced they were sharp absorbers of information, we sent them off to school with high hopes. Then we were forced to rethink some of our pat theories.

Before we left Europe, Martha spent the first month of grade one in a military school. For the next month, we were traveling. In November she enrolled in a Texas school. Her military teacher had assured us that she would encounter no difficulties.

"They don't really get down to work for the first couple of months in the first grade," she told us.

Obviously this teacher had never taught in San Antonio schools. From the start, Martha was lost. The other students were already reading, while she hardly knew how to identify the letters of the alphabet.

On the third day, I scheduled a conference with her teacher. "She's so far behind, she'll never catch up," the young woman announced.

Taken aback but not willing to concede defeat, I suggested, "Why not let her father and me give it a try? Let's see how impossible the situation really is."

That afternoon, I carried home an armload of ditto sheets and a new appreciation for the role of the family in education. During the next weeks we were to dismiss forever the theory that all learning takes place in classrooms. Every night Martha spent two hours with her daddy and the ditto sheets. Patiently, he drilled her on phonics and laid out rows of toy blocks to explain basic mathematical principles to her.

Each night our six-year-old fell into bed exhausted and had to be dragged out the next morning. She spent six hours in the classroom, then trudged home. Again she and her daddy went at the books. Day by day, the process was grueling. Would we discourage her forever from wanting to learn? What sort of a start was this?

Within a couple of months we had our answer. She had nearly caught up with her peers. By the end of the school year she had been promoted from the lowest reading group into the middle one, and she was reading daily from her King James Bible.

We enjoyed a rewarding sequel to the story five years later. I asked her sixth grade teacher why Martha never brought work home.

"She applies herself in class while many of the others are fooling around," he explained. "She's an excellent student, you know."

I related to him, then, the trauma of her "unfortunate" beginning. Wonder registered on his face, and he replied, "Unbelievable!"

Through the years of family living, we have seen that even institutional learning can be strengthened when supplemented by family involvement projects.

When Walt enrolled in a photography course at a local junior college, Tim arranged to take a similar seventh grade course. That was the beginning of an exciting, new, father-son adventure in learning. Together Walt and Tim spent dozens of hours experimenting, learning techniques of good picture taking, film processing, and printing. As a result, Tim progressed much faster than his fellow students. His special interest and expertise have opened many doors of unusual opportunity for him ever since.

For years our girls had begged me to teach them to sew. "When you take sewing in school, then I'll let you use my machine," I had told them. Martha had not been in the class long when she began making rather complicated garments. I commented one day on how quickly she was learning. "You must have a super teacher," I said.

She smiled. "Actually, Mother," she confided, "the teacher has taught me very little. I've learned most of what I know by watching you sew my clothes all these years."

Today, both of our girls work independently and creatively to make most of their own clothes.

One of the most rewarding areas of involvement for me has been volunteer aid work. As soon as Mary Jane started school, I was invited to enroll as a VIP—Voluntarily Involved Parent. Eager to keep my eye on what went on where my children were being educated, I accepted. Ever since, I have been helping in the classroom, on field trips, in the library, tutoring small groups in writing techniques. As a result, I have learned that both administrators and teachers can be very open to parental input. I have come to understand and appreciate a bit better the education process, and I have decided that it pays never to let ourselves remain strangers to the people who educate our children.

Walt and I have even found ourselves, from time to time, back in the classroom as students. We have learned a new appreciation for the many benefits offered by formal education at every growing stage of life.

But our children have enticed us beyond the school systems, vocational programs, and other organized plans into some indescribably exciting avenues of learning through involvement with each other in the family.

One Christmas season, I decided to give an evening coffee for some of my special friends. Schoolteachers, writers, volunteer parents, church friends, and family—all had so much in common, yet few of them knew each other. Further, I had been searching for a way to share with them how much the Christ of Christmas meant to me. What could be better than to bring them all together in a cozy, holiday atmosphere?

However, I lost my enthusiasm when I thought of all the work this would involve—dozens of cookies and fancy breads to bake, extra cleaning to do, invitations to write, a program to plan. How could I ever do it?

Then my fourteen-year-old daughter spoke up. "Please do it, Mother," she begged, "and let me help."

In the days that followed, both girls pitched in with the cooking, the cleaning, the invitation writing.

On the night of the coffee, I sat reveling in the low light shed by a gala assortment of candles the girls and I had collected. I felt an almost magical warmth throbbing through our living room. Silence flowed into the corners and blended with the soft voice of a friend as she shared a Christmas poem with the group. I glanced across the room at my own two daughters and realized that in the past few weeks they had taught me a priceless lesson in learning and living. Together, we had experienced the significant educational value of a shared family project.

Other kinds of work have drawn us closer to each other and expanded our learning horizons as well. Such undertakings as eradicating the burr clover from our lawns, rebuilding the VW engine, finishing the shell of our house addition. We have learned to do things we never dreamed could fit into the range of our potentials.

We have also discovered education taking place through the open exchange of ideas. In my letters sent home to the grandparents during our Air Force days, I find some rare gems. Recently, while browsing through these personal family archives, I discovered this intriguing entry:

> Martha has reached a stage of real curiosity about the where-froms of all the things she eats. "Mommy, what do cereals grow on? What do carrots grow on?" . . . When I try to tell her, she gets so excited and then pleads, "Mommy, please tell me that story again."

In more recent times, the maturity level of our idea interchanges has risen considerably. Discussions now center on politics, the arts, career planning, and some of the deeper aspects of Christian life and doctrine. But always the questions asked and the opinions expressed force us to stretch our minds, to reach ever outward, to grow and learn, to continue our education.

Undoubtedly the most effective method our children have found for continuing our education is to grab us by the hand and lead us forcibly into brand-new experiences.

When Walt and Tim built their darkroom, I was pleased to think of the opportunities it would provide for the two of them to work together. But I had no interest in photography myself. "Too complicated," I insisted.

Then one evening Tim bolted into my room, where I was reading. "Mom," he said, "you've just got to come and see what I made for you."

I followed his eager lead into the darkroom sanctuary. Here he showed me an enlarged print of a single rosebud. "I made it for your poetry notebook. Do you like it?" he asked, his voice replete with an achiever's pride.

At his urging, I stayed and watched the printing of several more pictures. To my surprise, I actually found the process quite intriguing.

Similarly, I never cared about drama until our girls began to show an interest in high school plays. Now, through day-by-day reports on after-school rehearsals, I have been learning a lot about dramatic techniques and production problems. Naturally, Walt and I both attend the performances. Little by little, our two daughters have opened up for us yet another door to learning.

As I thought about these two incidents, a sudden question jolted me: I wonder how many other exciting, life-enriching, and educational adventures I have missed in life because I yielded to natural inclinations and said no when my children have tried to coax me into other exciting, new, learning adventures?

A quarter of a century has passed since I reached that first anticipated educational milestone, high school graduation. I have enjoyed my hard-earned freedom from compulsory education ever since. But I have not stopped learning yet. My children have seen to that. Nor do I ever want to stop. In fact I am now thanking God that learning takes a lifetime, as well as all of eternity. And that school is never out!

SUGGESTED READING

Clarkson, E. Margaret. *Susie's Babies.* Grand Rapids: Eerdmans, 1960.

Tastefully and clearly done, this charming book introduces basic family-life concepts to the third or fourth grader. *Chats with Young Adults on Growing Up* (Eerdmans, 1962), a helpful sequel for early adolescents, deals with moral angles of sex education.

Fritz, Dorothy Bertolet. *Ways of Teaching.* Philadelphia: Westminster, 1965.

In this Christian education textbook, Dorothy Fritz's observations, analyses, and concrete suggestions speak to parents as well as teachers. If you are anxious to sharpen your teaching skills as a parent, this book with its easy-to-follow, logical philosophy and practical suggestions is valuable.

Frost, Gerhard E. *Bless My Growing.* Minneapolis: Augsburg, 1974.

Honest growing pains expressed by a seminary professor of Christian education. You'll enjoy the penetration of his ideas and the beauty of this illustrated book, which is a work of commendable art.

Taylor, Kenneth. *Almost Twelve.* Wheaton: Tyndale, 1972.

Recommended for a clinical treatment of the facts of life. Beautifully illustrated in black and white, and simply written, it also handles scriptural moral viewpoint clearly and concisely.

10

Wonder Moments Are for Sharing

The first year I tried to extend my writing schedule through the summer vacation, I posted on my door a sign that read:

DO NOT DISTURB
before 10 A.M.
I love you all!

In a special briefing session, I explained to our eleven-, twelve-, and fourteen-year-olds, "This means no interruptions, except for an emergency or something *really* important."

One morning, as I pecked away at my typewriter, I heard a bang of the kitchen screen and the flutter of excited voices. Suddenly my bedroom door flew open.

"Mommy, this is *really* important!"

Two elated youngsters rushed to my desk. Tim held out a tightly closed fist. Then, slowly, he opened it to reveal a tiny garden toad not half an inch long.

"It's our very first garden toad!" Mary Jane announced.

Really important, did they say? I ran a quick mental review. The whole family had been watching for this little fellow since the day in spring when several pairs of mating toads had filled our fish pond. For weeks we had protected the eggs and hatching polliwogs from fish and cats. Growing toads had become a major family concern.

Yes, I decided, this was a *really* important interruption. Whereupon I turned from the typewriter to share with my children a priceless moment of wonder.

Throughout the years of growing together in our family, we have learned a lot about what we like to call wonder moments. To us, a wonder moment is the instant when the human spirit makes a treasured discovery of mysterious beauty, majesty, power, or pleasure. It reminds me of a child attempting to gather all the secrets of the universe into his arms at once and hug them to his bosom.

To each of us, wonder moments come in diverse ways. Martha had one when her mama cat gave birth to four kittens. Mary Jane experienced wonder the day she saw a uniformed nurse in the supermarket. Tim captured such a moment when his newly built kite actually flew. Both the men in our family find unparalleled wonder in framing a breathtaking landscape or seascape in the viewfinder of a camera. I discover wonder moments regularly in the exchange of ideas and insights with some special friend by telephone or over a cup of tea. To my mother, a wonder moment consists of spending an afternoon splashing through the surf in bare feet and rolled-up pants' legs. Many of Great-Grandma's choice wonder moments happen on a televised football field or basketball court. Mom Herr's wonder becomes evident when I place a basket of fresh, steaming cornbread on the dinner table.

But the wonder moments that enrich our lives at the deepest levels and color our memories most vividly are often those we share in families.

While I was in the primary grades, we lived in a small town that had a busy railroad. The track ran almost through our backyard. My younger brother and I were intrigued by the dozens of trains that passed our home daily. We pretended to be trains. As we skated over the sidewalk cracks, our wheels made a rhythmic, click-click sound. Often we rode the train to Grandma's house in the big city.

We experienced many wonder moments with those old

steam trains. But one such moment made a particularly strong impression on me. I recall the whole family standing on the sloping grade of the railroad crossing as we waited and listened for a truly historical event. Our first electric railroad crossing signal had just been installed and was to perform upon the approach of the train scheduled to arrive any minute.

Then we heard it—a faint whistle coming closer. Seconds later the bright crossing lights flashed red and the bells began to ring. I nearly burst with wonder.

Many years afterward, I experienced another railroad wonder moment. This new encounter, experienced in company with my husband and children, brought the earlier wonder back. The sharing provided an added dimension.

We were driving through central Germany in the gorgeous fall season. Having discarded the road maps to meander among the hills and enjoy the scenery, we were in no particular rush to reach our destination.

Turning a corner into a tiny, storybook valley, we spotted cottony clouds of steam billowing up ahead of us. With sudden delight, we discovered in the valley below a shiny, black steam engine like the antiquated locomotive my brother and I had watched and imitated at play so many years earlier. Ringing its bell and blowing its whistle, the little iron horse chugged and puffed magnificently down the track, with its load of bright red freight cars in tow.

As the wonder of that moment grabbed me and held me tight, I shouted to my three little ones in the back seat, "Oh, kids, look! That's what trains looked like when Daddy and I were little!"

Though all three children had long since tired of watching swirling leaves and mountainscapes, they now awakened to the new thing before them. Together, four of us squealed and shouted our delight, while Daddy climbed out of the car and snapped two precious, irreplaceable slides.

That day we made one more deposit in our memory bank of priceless wonders. And I recognized that nothing could surpass a wonder moment relived with a new generation.

We have had other kinds of wonder moments too. Many nature-inspired ones have surprised us on long bicycle rides and hikes. We have watched and wondered at golden sunrises on a pond, the antics of giant polar bears in a zoo, fireworks of a spring thundershower, ice-crystallized trees, and many more.

Family cultural ventures also bring us wonder. On a school field-trip Martha and I shared our first visit to the San Francisco Opera House. So many artistic things caught our attention that day—the immensity and ornate intricacy of the building, the fascination and beauty of the live symphony performance, the world-famous city itself.

We have stocked our memory banks with generous supplies of wonder on visits to art galleries, stage plays, atmosphered restaurants, Disneyland, libraries, Gothic churches, and a good many other works of man-made art.

We have also known moments of rare personal wonder—the kind that reach us by way of the heart. These we create for one another with planned precision or enthusiastic spontaneity. It seems to me that children possess a special aptitude for producing these kinds of inspiration.

One day I felt discouraged about something. Because I am not adept at hiding my feelings, the whole family detected my mood. Toward evening I found a small envelope on my desk. Inside was the following note penned on a piece of personalized stationery:

> **Mom,**
>   Just to let you know I care, even though I don't completely understand.
>   **Love,**
>   Your Daughter

This simple act of loving concern reminded me of a magazine advertisement that said, "Life is too short and winter's too long to go without mink." That life is short, and much of its climate is wintry, I knew very well, particularly on that day and in my gray mood. I also sensed that in families we provide each other with mink coats for the long winter—not just fur for warmth, but mink—warmth with a touch of luxury and memorability.

Of all the wonder moments we share with our children, the most precious are the spiritual experiences of worshipful response to a living, personal Father-God. In earlier years, our toddlers thrilled us with simple statements such as, "Jesus is the boss of us, and I love Him." Through the passing years, expressions have matched the children's growth in maturity.

About a year and a half ago, Martha and I drove along a quiet city street one evening. "Mom," she spoke with a sudden burst of revelation, "I've just thought of something gorgeous. The beauty of our Christian faith is that we have the kind of God everybody wants. But nobody but a Christian dares to believe that such a God exists." The inner glow of her worshiping person shone through and turned that into a choice moment of sublime, spiritual wonder.

I am beginning to read the Scriptures, now, with a lookout for examples of men and women enjoying wonder moments with their God. The Bible is packed with them.

One of my favorites is Psalm 8:1: "O LORD, our Lord, how majestic is Thy name in all the earth." I also caught a glimpse of a special wonder moment in the gospels when I read that Peter once followed Jesus' seemingly impractical orders and came up with a record catch of fish. I imagined him and the other disciples tugging away at those nets overcrowded with slippery, squirming, wriggling, silver fish. What a fantastic sort of wonder moment they all celebrated!

Suddenly Peter, overwhelmed with the superiority of his Lord, bowed low before Jesus and exclaimed with wonder, "Depart from me; for I am a sinful man" (Luke 5:8, KJV).

At this point in our family journey toward maturity, we are seeing that Jesus often urges His followers into deeper involvements, ventures of risk, and revolutionized attitudes. Whenever we accept His challenge, something happens—in God and in us. He actually enjoys each new, really important moment with us. In return, He enriches our lives with fresh viewpoints and plateaus of significant growth. After all, who knows better than He that wonder moments are for sharing?

SUGGESTED READING

Carson, Rachel. *The Sense of Wonder.* N.Y.: Harper & Row, 1956.

Here is a beautiful, 95-page book of words and photographs to inspire parents, aunts, grandparents, and teachers to take our children by the hand and accompany them into the discoveries of wonder. Text is brief and practical in its suggestions.

Gordon, Arthur. *A Touch of Wonder.* Old Tappan: Revell, 1974.

Subtitled *A Book to Help People Stay in Love with Life,* this beautiful volume is one of the inspirational and literary gems of modern writing. Arthur Gordon, editor of *Guideposts,* writes with a golden pen, simply, and directly to the heart. Wonder moments are guaranteed to accompany the reading of this book around the family circle—one chapter at a time, either in order or at random.

Schaeffer, Edith. *Hidden Art.* Wheaton: Tyndale, 1971.

For the artist or would-be artist/parent looking for ways to add a touch of art to everyday family living, this book provides a magnificent guide. Mrs. Schaeffer convinces the most inartistic of us that we can practice family art. She shows us how to turn mundane activities and places into delightful and educational experiences of wonder.

Part 3

FIXING VALUES: A SET OF GUIDELINES

My husband's salary places us in a solid middle-income bracket. We eat well, stay warm, visit the orthodontist, even drive two cars part of the time. And I have never had to go to work outside the home.

In today's inflationary society, however, this never leaves room for the degree of affluence that many of our children's friends enjoy. When they were little, our three used to compare their situation with the others. Often they became unhappy and wished for more of the material things they saw that their friends had.

One day Martha complained to me, "Mommy, why can't I have as many pretty clothes as Suzanne?"

The question was not simple to answer. Her daddy and I didn't want her to feel the pain of responsibility for her material well-being—not yet. At ten, she was too young to handle such a heavy dose of care about life. On the other hand, we could not afford to lavishly provide for all her expensive whims. Not only did our budget not allow for the extravagance, neither did her character development.

"There are a couple of ways we could go about getting more nice clothes for you," I suggested. "First, we could stop giving any money to the church. That amounts to quite a bit— enough to buy a lot of beautiful dresses."

I paused and watched the look of questioning displeasure wrinkle its way across her brow and sober her blue eyes.

"Oh, no, Mommy. We can't do that," she said deliberately.

"Well, then," I went on, "the second possibility is for me to go get a job. Lots of mothers do, you know. Probably even Suzanne's."

She responded instantly, "Then you'd never be here when I come home from school. I know. Suzanne's mother never is."

"Is that more important than new clothes?" I asked.

Throwing her arms around my neck, she smiled and said emphatically, "That's more important than anything!"

The teaching of values is difficult in a culture that has erased many of the clear, bold outlines once drawn for us by our parents. We have found it equally difficult to hold on to those values ourselves. The daily routine of family interrelationships often pressures us to question all we learned back home.

In the family circle, however, we are also finding the reaffirmation and enlightenment needed to help us sort the good from the bad and establish our own set of divinely ordered value guidelines for growth.

Through our parenting vocation, we are be-

ginning to distinguish absolutes from vari-
ables, to take time out for living, to let a thing
be a thing, and to define that often threatening
word, *success.*

11

Time Out for Living

"Dear God, even an ulcer might be better than this," I prayed, staring in my mirror at eyes circled from frustration. Convinced I couldn't face another day, I added, "At least, I'd get some rest that way."

The trouble had grown out of a decision Walt and I had made when he left the service two years earlier. After twelve years of military regimentation and financial security, we were on our own. The Lord had provided Walt with a promising job in electronics, his special field.

Then, just as we prepared to move on, a persuasive salesman came our way. He distributed our favorite brand of soap and eagerly shared with us the joys and added financial security of a family-owned-and-operated business. "Excellent supplementary income! Beautiful way to get acquainted in a new community! Great family project!"

Excited with the prospects, we signed on the dotted line and bought our kits. We hoped only to do a small amount of business. But as we worked at it those first months, and our sponsor's promises began to materialize, we enlarged our dreams. Then we enlisted some new distributors with unlimited ambitions for success. Now being pushed from behind, pulled from ahead, and threatened by a declining economy (layoffs in the electronic industry plagued our area), we were forced to accelerate our own pace. This was when our dreams began turning into nightmares.

Walt's regular work duties increased rapidly during that period. The heaviest load of the business fell on me. Telephone calls, deliveries, sales meetings, neighborhood canvassing, book work—the whole thing escalated into a full-time race. At the same time, I held several important leadership positions at church and served as a parent volunteer worker at school.

Business had never been my first love, but I soon learned to enjoy it. At first, our children were excited about the idea; they even helped distribute literature and sell soap. Gradually their attitude changed. One night as I rushed them into their pajamas before a sales meeting to be held in our living room, one of them spoke up. "Mommy, why do you always have to have all these dumb sales meetings?" That was the beginning of a protest that was to become increasingly loud.

I also noticed that I was changing. Business activities sapped my energy so that I rarely had any left over for the family. I nagged at Walt and the children. My temper ran consistently short. At the cross of an eye, I would burst into tears. Our marriage relationship grew tenuous. I almost lost my ability to pray. My journal of those days is filled with pain, struggle, and a constant plea with God to "restore unto me the joy of my salvation."

On that memorable morning before my mirror, I had reached the end of my tether. I wrestled with several irreconcilable fears. Walt and I both felt we did not dare give up our business just then. All around us, men were being laid off their jobs. It could happen to us, too. If we cut our ties with the business, where would we turn? Besides, we had committed ourselves to excel. What would our friends say if we quit? And our sponsor? He was constantly reminding us, "Anybody who's not afraid of work can make a go of this business."

On the other hand, what would happen if we went on

this way? Desperate for relief from the pressures, I knew something had to be done.

As so often happens, God had already been preparing an effective set of circumstances to answer my prayer. Looking back now, I see three incidents—standing out above all the others—that evidence His masterful planning.

First, during the sales meetings, rallies, and training sessions of the next few weeks, I began to detect some implications of the business philosophy that disturbed me —things I had missed before.

"Give the business all you have for one full year." I had heard it before. But now I saw what it involved. Give up your church work and community services. Explain to your children that this is your year to grow. They will survive without you!

So those were the stakes! Suddenly, for the first time, the big picture emerged from fuzzy fantasy to stark reality. "Does this mean," I asked in disbelief, "that I am expected to ignore my children for one whole year?"

"Oh, but they'll adjust." Everybody knew the line. "When you explain to them that it's only temporary, and that it's the only way to bring financial prosperity to your family, they'll be more than happy to make do. In fact, they'll be glad to help."

I understood now why Martha, Tim, and Mary Jane had come to hate the very name of the soap company we had become entangled with. Clearly they saw my priority system: *Full-time* saleswoman, *part-time* church woman, and *spare-time* wife and mother. In their childlike ways they had been begging me to give up what they saw as a rival interest and return to *full-time* motherhood.

Once I saw the issue, I knew what I must do. Though I realized it would mean disappointing the people who had invested effort and money in my training, I had no doubt that I must start being fair to my family. I admitted that I had been a spare-time mother long enough. The time had come to put my husband and children first, where they belonged.

From that moment on, I knew the business was on its way out. But with the shaky economy and Walt's hesitation about total severance of our ties, I was not yet free to do what my heart and my children wanted me to do.

That summer, event number two took place. We loaded our VW station wagon with camping gear and pitched our huge orange tent in a wilderness campground in the high Sierras of Yosemite National Park. Here our children coaxed us into a different sort of existence—the relaxed, time-out-for-rest-and-each-other kind.

The luxury of sleeping late in a fragrant pine forest, where bluejays chattered and squirrels dropped their nut husks on the tent roof—we had almost forgotten it could happen. Never had bonfires seemed so cheerful, so personal. Each hike up a dome, through the woods, into the mist of a full waterfall began to clear my mind of the cobwebs spun by balanced accounts and customer calls. I discovered an almost magical power in moving water. The creek that flowed past our tent; the river that meandered through high-altitude meadows and thundered down the canyons; the sparkling, shore-slapping lakes; those tremendous waterfalls—each performed an act of healing for my collapsing nerves.

Every detail of that special vacation performed a service to our family. For the first time in months—or was it years?—we enjoyed talking, playing, laughing, relaxing, and just being together. We all came home convinced that life was more than schedules, duties, routines—and soap!

We were now ready for circumstance number three. As I began to relax after that mountain camping trip, I experienced some strange stomach pains, a constant nagging hunger, and a marked reduction in energy levels. I remembered that prayer about an ulcer and finally voiced another, "Lord, please don't let this be a real ulcer. But could You make it something bad enough to give me an excuse to sever my ties with the business, say no to a lot of demanding people, and get some long overdue rest?"

Within a week I had my answer. My doctor diagnosed my stomach problems as preulcer symptoms. She prescribed medication, a bland diet, and *lots of rest*. At the same time, Walt received a pay raise equal to our average business income (slumping economy notwithstanding). Our fear of leaving a secure source of emergency income lost its last major basis for power and all but died.

We made a family celebration out of packing away the soap trappings that had cluttered our kitchen, our living area, and our lives for much too long.

At first, I felt awkward and restless taking long afternoon rests and staying home nights. The results, though, were luxurious. They brought healing to me as a person and to our bruised family organism.

Often as I lay on the couch, half dozing through those cozy afternoons, I recalled other relaxed days of the past. Earlier days had brought precious hours shared with the children—leisurely strolling to the park to watch the fuzzy ducklings scoot across the water in a line behind their proud mother; sipping colored-water tea with a six-year-old hostess; flying a newspaper kite with a robust lad who giggled contagiously; rocking a dolly to sleep while her youthful mother swept the floor with deliberate efficiency.

Once more my memories enticed me to throw open the doors and let these same children, now a few years older, lead me into restful hours, pastimes filled with play, even journeys into literary fantasy. Together, we oiled the hinges on the game cupboard and dug out the longtime favorite puzzles, checkers, badminton, dominoes, and many other games we had forgotten.

We reinstated those treasured library visits; we renewed acquaintances with some long-neglected, special friends and met a circle of new ones. Once more, we put a "reserved" tag on many of the Saturdays of our calendar and set off to explore the special fascinations of our northern California bay area.

A new set of attitudes and habit patterns also emerged during those months of restoration. Since the children were little, I had always prodded them to "hurry up and dress," "hurry up and eat," "hurry up and get ready; we're going to be late." Now I found even I couldn't face life with a "hurry up" philosophy anymore. If my nerves were to heal and stay healed, I must learn the art of that childlike life-style known as leisureliness. Among other things, this meant lying in bed for ten to fifteen minutes after the alarm sounded each morning. I learned to use this time for stretching, yawning, meditating, praying, exchanging unrushed greetings and good-morning kisses with my husband. I came to appreciate the Chinese explanation for this sort of therapeutic laziness as an opportunity for the soul to catch up with the body before our day begins.

I have found that this simple, relaxation exercise goes a long way in preparing me to cope with each challenge of the day in a spirit of leisure. Not that the hectic moments have stopped coming. But at least I am learning to handle them when they do.

Some time after we parted company with the soap, the children and I sat in the car outside Walt's shop one afternoon and waited for him to join us. One of Walt's co-workers dropped by to chat a few minutes.

"So you've given up the business, eh?" he asked.

Before I could reply, I heard an enthusiastic voice from

the back seat: "She sure did! And we have a real mother again!"

That was when I realized how great a part our three little ones had played in the reordering of our lives. Without being aware of the fantastic truths themselves, they had reached out with childlike simplicity and winsomeness to teach us that rest is part of activity, play is part of work, sleep is part of growth, stopping is part of going, and meditation is part of communication—all truths the Lord has clearly outlined for us in the Scriptures:

"Come ye yourselves apart . . . and rest awhile" (Mark 6:31, KJV).

"Be still, and know that I am God" (Psalm 46:10, KJV).

"They that wait upon the LORD shall renew their strength" (Isaiah 40:31, KJV).

"Rest in the Lord" (Psalm 37:7, KJV).

Today I am so glad the Lord uses families to illustrate and effectively communicate to us these important messages. As the children have grown older, we have watched them slip into some of the same busy patterns that so easily trapped us. At times I have to remind them of the unpleasant consequences of overcommitment during the days when I ran a business, sang in the church choir, led the women's missionary society, worked three days a week in the school library, and studied writing. They remember all too well. Each time I repeat the story, I realize afresh that my example of taking time out to live in the childlike ways they have taught me will always be as essential to their survival as to my own.

SUGGESTED READING

Walker, Georgiana, ed. *The Celebration Book*. Glendale, Cal.: Regal, 1977.

In this practical collection of fun things to do in families, Christian parents share the why and how of family celebrations. The book contains inspirational articles and ideas (many complete with patterns and detailed directions) for turning common days and holidays into treasured memories and/or enduring family traditions.

12

A Thing Is a Thing—Or Is It?

John, our close GI friend in Europe, was an artist. Several months before our foreign duty tour ended, he told us, "I want to paint you a picture. A Dutch scene that's different from the usual. Something to bring back warm memories."

We searched a whole summer for a canvas. Finally, in a remote city far to the north, we found just the unique piece we wanted—a white oval china platter with an intricate, gold leaf border. Then we sorted through dozens of slides and chose a favorite.

John painted the canalside pastoral scene in brilliant oils. We brought our prized possession home to America and displayed it prominently on the living room coffee table. For the next two years we admired this special work of art and reveled in the memories it evoked.

Then, in an instant of exuberance, one of the children (happily, I have forgotten which one) jostled the plate atop its slippery pedestal. Our family treasure slid to the hardwood floor and shattered into a hundred, unsalvageable pieces.

Hurt, disappointed, angry, I opened my mouth to lash out against the child's clumsiness. Didn't he realize the value of this thing he had so carelessly destroyed? Perhaps if he had been raised during the depression as his father and I had, he would understand and be more cautious. We had learned the hard way that things never came easily, and that they were worth caring for, saving, and respecting.

One glance at the little one, weeping and trembling with fear, checked my outburst long enough for him to plead for mercy.

"Oh, Mommy, I didn't mean to—it was a accident—I so sorry!"

As the cowering child backed off from me, I remembered having read in a magazine, several years before, never to spank a child when he breaks something accidentally. His own guilt is sufficient punishment. This had always seemed a rather permissive position. Now, it began to make sense.

Another set of words came into focus now, too. "A man's life consisteth not in the abundance of the things which he possesseth" (Luke 12:15, KJV). I had memorized the words in my childhood. Often this verse and its implications had soothed the pain I felt at not having as many nice things as some neighbor friends. It had also helped me learn to share my toys and tithe any allowance or earnings I might enjoy.

As parents, Walt and I both found the application of this truth to be painful at times. Whenever one of the children tore a page from a favorite book, scribbled across the wallpaper, or defaced a piece of furniture, he challenged our value system once more.

Walt always whipped out a ready answer. At each encounter with material tragedy, he would sigh and repeat, "My grandmother always said, 'If you have kids, you can't have anything else.'" What a noble concept! It was one we could embrace with philosophical piety once the emotional moment had passed. After all, we would reason, which is more important—children or possessions?

But what about now, standing numbly in the middle of my living room as fragments of a china-and-oils treasure lay at my feet? My emotional moment still burned hot. Could I really accept either Christ's words or Grandma's old adage?

Another glance at the guilty child, still weeping and cowering, told me that both Jesus and Walt's grandmother had been right. I opened my arms, and my child bounded into them. For awhile we wept together. At last, drawing on all the resources of divine grace I could grasp, I said, "It's going to be all right, honey. Mommy should have kept the plate in a safer place."

To this day, remembering our Dutch plate still hurts. But the memory brings a much clarified understanding of the old axiom: a thing is a thing. Experience is helping us to add that we must therefore hold things loosely lest in losing a thing we lose a part of ourselves.

We are also learning that though a thing may be only a thing, it does have some justifiable value. Hence the need to learn thriftiness.

We taught our children that "every good . . . and perfect gift is from above" (James 1:17, KJV) . Then, at times, we tried to persuade them to part with some of the treasured things they had been collecting. "God doesn't like to see a mess, so we must get rid of the junk," we told them.

Here we hit some snags. Tim's definition of junk and ours have always clashed. While he was in kindergarten, he made daily raids on the neighborhood gutters and stashed away his marvelous finds in an already-too-small bedroom. Once a week I invaded the room with a large trash barrel. Amazingly, I got away with this for quite awhile.

As he grew older and his collections grew more sophisticated, I began keeping his door closed. Once a month or so, I made him dig through the accumulated clutter and eliminate a lot of trivia.

One such Saturday morning I announced, "OK, son. Time to clear out the junk."

"I don't have any junk," he shot back.

"Then what do you call these things?" I stooped over a rickety cart having three sides that didn't quite meet at the corners, and lifted out a piece of wrinkled, blue construction paper, a handful of empty gum wrappers, and a half-deflated balloon.

"They're my treasures," he defended.

"Treasures?" I taunted.

"Gonna use 'em for somethin'—someday!"

I handed him a paper bag for his trash and gave him a deadline for completion of the project—"or no baseball." Heading for the door, I was halted by the winsome plea, "But Mom—"

I turned and looked back over my shoulder at my dejected ten-year-old. Holding a broken kite stick, he sat on the edge of his bed. A look of intense pain spread across his freckled face.

"Just think of all the things I'm going to invent someday—with these very treasures!"

That frustrating interview with a chronic junk collector did something special for me. It freed me to admit that my own collections of fabric scraps, used envelopes, and plastic bags could be useful. I began looking at everything for its utilitarian potential before I tossed it out to the rubbish man. I learned to make patchwork garments, purses, and miscellaneous gift items. I even wrote an article for a Sunday school teachers' magazine. Titled "Save It; You'll Need It," the article described techniques for transforming discards into teaching tools.

We are now understanding that a thing is indeed a gift from God. Therefore we must use it responsibly, for He holds us accountable.

A very long time ago, Martha and her great-grandmother teamed up to begin to teach us yet another lesson concerning the relative values of things.

Martha's first doll was a hand-me-down from my childhood. Though well-preserved for her twenty-odd years, her wood-composition body began to disintegrate. Daddy repaired Susy, and repaired again, until he had to announce that her ailing joints could no longer be safely mended.

Two-year-old Martha could not quite accept the truth that Susy was gone.

Great-Grandma was visiting at the time. "Take me to the toy store," she insisted. "We're going to buy a new doll."

Enroute downtown she told me, "When I was a girl, I wanted a dolly of my own more than anything. But I never got one. No great-granddaughter of mine is going to live without a doll."

In the toy store, I watched with fascination as Grandma searched for just the right doll. As she moved about the doll department, exclaiming at all the pretty babies, her "little girl in the middle" was still obviously vibrant. With the extravagant taste of a child and never even glancing at the price tag, she chose one large, well-built, baby doll.

"But, Grandma," I protested, "this one is too expensive for you to buy."

"Nonsense," she countered. "Only the best will do. There is no price tag too high for my great-granddaughter."

Grandma glowed and wriggled with delight all the way home. We found Martha napping. Grandma tiptoed to the girl's bed and laid the new doll beside her. Then, hoping to hasten the waking process, she stood nearby, impatiently clearing her throat and making other subtle noises.

All the while I wondered if I had done right to let Grandma spend so much money. I knew she really couldn't afford this luxury.

Then Martha awoke. When I saw the look on Grandma's face as Martha laid eyes on her new treasure, I had my answer. There was not enough money in all the bank accounts of the world to pay for the joy Grandma registered in giving this special bit of her own childhood dreams—this *thing*—to her only great-granddaughter.

I began to recognize that a thing is often much more than a thing. Many times since, Walt and I have both observed the effect of things on the family, and our faith in this principle has been strengthened.

We have remembered it when three excited children lugged home armloads of teachers' discards on the last day of school; when Tim salvaged rough scraps of lumber to make a crude, wooden shoe box for his daddy; when Mary Jane made her first colonial costume from an old quilted bedspread and paraded the streets with elegance on Halloween night; when Martha stitched a hem in a piece of cloth, and then—because she couldn't wait another week for Christmas—she showed her daddy the hankie she had made for him. We recall the principle whenever we take the family out to the Spaghetti Factory, go shopping for a graduation dress, build a darkroom in the corner of the garage, or add on to our house to make room for Mom Herr to come live with us.

I especially remembered that a thing can be more than a thing the year we gave Mary Jane a lion puppet for her birthday. For years she had gotten first one kitten and then another. Yet she never managed to keep one for more than a few months. Each time we got her a new live pet, she had grown terribly attached to it. Then, within a matter of months, it would either die or disappear.

When she met Aslan the lion in C. S. Lewis's Narnia series, she began begging for a stuffed lion in place of the live pets she could not seem to keep. We searched the stores and found nothing short of a $100 specimen that stood eight feet tall. A little out of our spending bracket! So we settled for a hand puppet donated by a puppeteer friend.

At the neighborhood dime store, Mary Jane and I purchased long, silky fringe to make her Aslan a regal mane. From that day on, he accompanied her to school, to the table, to bed, to the bathroom, even as far as the church parking lot. At school he became a special favorite in the sixth grade class, where he performed as star in many puppet shows written and produced by students.

Then one day in midsummer, as Mary Jane and I returned home from the supermarket, she realized that her friend was missing.

"Oh, Mother," she wailed, "I left Aslan at the grocery store!"

He wasn't there when we went back to find him. He didn't show up in the lost and found. Our heartbroken daughter went into mourning.

We told her how sorry we felt about it. We tried to console her. "But he's only a toy, you know."

"Oh, no!" she protested. "He was like real!"

Walt and I reasoned that surely in time she would forget her loss. In the meantime we offered to find her another live kitten.

"He'll only die or run away," she lamented. "I want my Aslan back."

Now we understood why this puppet had meant so much to her. She must have felt a special security in owning Aslan, the pet who could not wander away or get sick and die. Sensing this deeper meaning to her grief, we reminded her that nothing in life is permanent. "Not the pets, or the toys, or even the people. But we can always remember the fun we had with Aslan and be happy about it."

How much good our advice did, we could not tell. Our girl's grief did seem to subside a bit. She even consented to start looking for a new, live kitten.

But before we found the kitten, another unexpected event occurred. Two months after the supermarket catastrophe, Mary Jane and I were passing through the checkout stand of the same grocery store. Mary Jane gasped and pointed toward the stack of empty boxes by the window.

"Mom," she shouted excitedly as she shoved her way

past me in the line. "Look who's up there on top of the box pile."

I looked up and saw Aslan, the lost puppet, smiling down at us as if he had just returned from an extended visit to Narnia, but was very happy to be home again.

No reunion of old friends was ever more joyous. Grabbing the puppet, Mary Jane hugged and kissed him and danced out the door with him. Big tears rolled down her cheeks and dampened Aslan's shiny, gold mane.

Once more her friend became her constant companion. This time, though, his glory was short-lived. When she took him to school, her peers informed her that puppets do not belong in junior high school. Within a week she had retired him to her pillow, where his major duty ever since has been to welcome her to dreamland each night. Also, we soon had a live, crying kitten in the house.

We never knew how or where Aslan spent those two months when he was separated from us, or how he found his way back to the box pile. But because he did, we were all able to evaluate our growth of understanding about the value of things. Mary Jane still loves Aslan. He will always be special to her, for he has helped her to preserve her little girl in the middle and also to handle the transitoriness of live pets and other things with greater maturity.

Is a thing always a thing? We have to admit that our children have taught us most aptly that it is often much more. If we are wise, we will not despise the potential of some thing to bring happiness. Nor will we forget that the true value of any thing is not in itself but in the pleasure and learning it brings, the growth it fosters, the memories it evokes, and the family relationships it helps to build.

13

What Is Success?

In the seventh grade, Mary Jane wrote a play based on one of her favorite Gothic novels. Her English teacher, anxious to see her develop her literary talent, had encouraged the venture. The finished project pleased us all.

"Let's give your play to the drama teacher," Mrs. E. suggested. "I'll bet she'd like to give it to her drama class to produce next year."

All summer, Mary Jane planned how she would help direct her play. Mentally she cast it, dreamed of staging and properties, and anticipated the fall, when her successful work of art could be displayed for the whole school and part of the community.

With the opening of school, Mary Jane conferred with the drama teacher and the play began to take shape. Her excitement mounted steadily until one afternoon in late November. I first heard of the trouble when, in a stormy rage, she burst into the house after school.

"It isn't fair!" she exploded. "The drama class isn't going to do my play after all. Mrs. R. says it's too hard."

I stood by in awkward silence. What could I say? Ever since this child was old enough to reason, I had been waging a strong campaign to convince her she was not a failure in life just because she failed while trying to do something.

Whenever she had come home with a single C on her report card and demanded to know why she couldn't get all A's and B's, I had asked simply, "Did you do your best?"

"Yes, Mother," was usually her answer.

"Then don't fret. Success is not winning every time. Success is always doing your best."

Our youngest child's frustrations arose mostly from not being able to do all the things her older sister could do so well.

"You're three years younger than Martha," I reminded her repeatedly. "Wait awhile. But keep trying." She did try, and sometimes even surpassed her big sister in accomplishments.

But this play fit into a special category. It was Mary Jane's own thing. Even Martha had never written and helped produce a play. Here was little sister's big chance. And it had failed.

Sensing the futility of advice in that dark moment, I offered a simple "I'm sorry, dear" and tried to place my arm around her shoulder. She rebuffed me and seemed not to hear any attempt at consolation.

At last, in tears she stomped down the hall shouting, "But Mrs. R. promised—she promised—she promised."

For a long time I heard muffled sobs from the bedroom at the back corner of the house. But by the next morning, most of her bitterness had disappeared. "I knew all along that it wasn't going to work," she said with a sigh. How much of her analysis was cover for deep hurts, and how much was evidence of a growing maturity, we could not be sure.

In the weeks that followed, though, we watched with awe and pride a surprising development in our thirteen-year-old's maturing process. With fresh determination, she began to pick up the pieces of her broken dreams and to recycle them. In her eighth grade English class, under the inspiring prodding of another wise teacher, she collaborated with a friend to write a second play. They entered it in a contest sponsored by a nearby children's theater group and startled themselves by winning first place out of thirty-five entries from around the country.

Later, sitting in the Palo Alto Children's Theatre, we watched our daughter and her friend receive their cash award, and we glowed with pride over this success. Then I wondered if she had really failed with the first play. Or would this play have been a failure if it had lost the contest? I began to ask myself once more the question which had passed through my mind so many times over the years: *What is success?*

Several of my favorite Bible verses told me how to achieve success. "This book of the law shall not depart from your mouth, but you shall meditate on it day and night, so that you may be careful to do according to all that is written in it; for then you will make your way prosperous, and then you will have success" (Joshua 1:8). I recalled also the blessed man of Psalm 1; because he walks righteously and meditates both day and night in the Law of God, "in whatever he does, he prospers" (Psalm 1:3).

I used to consider this to be a sort of magic formula—obey God's words and He will see to it that everything you do succeeds. Experience helped me understand, though, that this was not the real meaning of those verses. No matter how hard I prayed or how faithfully I obeyed, I still met with many inexplicable failures.

In the complexity of family relationships and daily living, we are beginning to find the warmth and strength of some workable and realistic profiles of success. And we are also finding that these square with the total teaching of Scripture.

In the soap-selling business, we learned that success begins with setting right goals. These goals must fit us, not our supervisor with his success kits and mass training programs.

For me at least, Tim's adventures in athletics amplified

this idea. Through one important incident, I learned that finding the goal that fits often means trying on several likely ones for size. Through the medium of success and failure we can select goals that fit and best express our personalities.

We are an unathletic family. But in the fourth grade, Tim decided to break the pattern and play Little League baseball. For a long time, he found the challenge difficult. His biggest problem was to hit the ball.

One afternoon he came running home from practice with some exciting news. "Mom, I hit the ball and got all the way to first base."

I opened my mouth to congratulate him, but he went on: "It didn't count, though. It was a foul ball."

"That's still great news." I tried to encourage him. "At least you hit it. All you have to do now is to practice straightening out your hits."

A couple of days later, Tim found me in a low mood. I had been working hard at my writing in recent months. But I had received nothing more than returned manuscripts and printed editorial rejection slips. Often I had decided to quit, only to find that I couldn't. Something inside pushed me on.

"What's the matter, Mom?" Tim asked me.

"Just a little discouraged about my writing," I told him. "Like you and your baseball. I work so hard at producing what I think is a great manuscript. Then I send it off flying. But it always ends up being a foul ball—aimed in the wrong direction."

With a manner that reminded me of the friendly, awkward, cocker spaniel puppy my brother once owned, my young son reached up and patted me on the arm. "Remember what you told me, Mom? Keep practicing and you'll learn to straighten them all out."

Tim played baseball for two seasons. He never made the

all-star team, but he did learn to straighten out most of his hits. Later, in his high school days, he found that cross-country racing fit him better than baseball.

I also took "our good advice" and went on writing. Before long, Tim's words turned out to be prophetic. A few letters of acceptance and welcome paychecks came slipping in between rejection slips.

In persisting even through my failures, and by redirecting my efforts, I was able to discover the kinds of writing that best fit me. This discovery released my potential for achievement, which is success in its visible, measurable form.

Parenting has also taught us that success is not always visible. In fact, many times we have felt certain we were failing, only to learn later that our greatest successes were actually being achieved. While we looked for one kind of success, some deeper, more important sort was going on beneath the stormy surface that tossed about our boat of confidence.

Walt and I have wrestled with a sense of failure in the area of finances perhaps more often than in any other. To begin with, money management is not our forte. Beyond this, we have decided that nothing can make a parent feel so unsuccessful as attempting to balance the family budget while providing adequately for three teenagers in today's affluent society. Not only is the money hard to come by, but the challenge of distinguishing between wants and needs has often convinced us that fiscal success is only a fairy tale.

Occasionally, though, one of our demanding teenagers will startle us with his mature insights and suggest to us that success is not always to be found where we expect it. It is often neither visible nor tangibly measurable.

Following a high school choral concert, Walt and I took Martha to a local pie house to celebrate her performance.

When we had finished our apple, cherry, and lemon meringue slices, Martha thanked her daddy for this rare treat.

"I wish I could do it more often," he responded, in a tone that said, "I apologize for not being a more successful parent-provider."

"You know, Daddy," Martha countered philosophically, "I don't really wish for that. When I'm honest, I know that if we did this more often, it wouldn't be special anymore."

Talk about adequate provision! In her inimitable way, our young teenager was trying to tell us that we didn't need to prove our success by making a million dollars or by giving her even half the pleasures she wanted. Instead, we show ourselves successful when we can unapologetically and enthusiastically live within our means.

One of the profoundest lessons we are all learning is that being successful involves putting persons before achievements, before material things, before schedules, sometimes before church activities—in fact, before everything but God Himself.

I think I would enjoy a neat orderly household, where every*thing* stays in its place, every*body* performs his duties, and every *activity* falls conveniently into its niche on the family calendar. However, I will never know for sure, for I don't live between the covers of *House Beautiful,* or in the TV family that has as many cars as drivers, or even in a double-income household.

After two decades of housewifery, I have conceded that some things in life are after all more important than an antiseptic house, a rigid schedule, and an obsession with discipline and duty.

This concession makes me feel only a little less ill at ease when my failure in these areas is exposed to some threatening, efficient soul who comes to visit.

One day recently, when a great many things had been removed from their places and lay in piles about the house, just such an unexpected guest arrived. With self-conscious lack of poise, I apologized for the mess.

As soon as the visitor left, Martha accosted me in a corner of the kitchen and scolded, "Mother, this house is *not* messy. Just lived in!"

Those two brief sentences gave me a whole new viewpoint on successful household management. I realized that success means creating a warm atmosphere that invites my family members to "come on in, kick off your shoes, learn to live and love and grow; for in this place, you are *number one.*"

The summer before her high school graduation, Martha took a baby-sitting job. For fifty hours a week she cared for a lively, eight-year-old girl. The child had had a variety of baby-sitters and gave her newest one quite a chase. She tested every possible channel for freedom. For the first time in her life, Martha came face to face with parental kinds of decisions.

Near the end of the summer, she confessed to me, "Mom, I used to wonder why you sometimes say you feel like a failure as a mother. Now I understand."

"Oh! How so?" I asked.

"Because there's just no way you can ever be sure you made the right decision, is there?"

"Not really," I answered.

I recalled how at that very moment, some of the books Martha and Mary Jane brought home from the library, some of their wardrobe selections, some of the TV movies they chose to watch, and the music all our children enjoyed frankly disturbed me. I knew that, as a domineering personality type, far too often I had tried to censor their involvements in these areas. Over and over they had to remind me, "Mom, we already know what you think; you don't need to tell us again."

And they were right. The values we had communicated

by word and life had provided all three of our children with a standard of life. The God we had led them to worship now went with them during these years when they were proving the old, familiar patterns and seeking to establish a Christian life-style of their own. Our intrusion in the process had often become a divisive nagging and a hindrance to growth.

Martha broke into my wandering thoughts, "But how can a parent ever measure his success?" she asked.

I could feel the deep concern in the heart of my teenager who'd played mother all summer.

"Good question," I admitted. Then I told her that recently I had read a relevant passage in Bruce Larson's *Living on the Growing Edge:* "Ultimately we never know whether we have succeeded . . . the will of God for us is not that we accomplish an objective, but that we attempt it."[1]

Finally, I summarized for Martha how I had come to feel that to succeed as a parent is to trust God and try our best to follow the wisdom He gives us. She smiled and finished for me: "And to fail is to quit trying."

Impulsively I hugged the blossoming woman who in her seventeen years had introduced me to so much learning. Suddenly I recognized that what I had taught her and her brother and sister about persisting through each failure was precisely what living with them had taught me about success in my own life—both as a person and as a parent.

Part 4

INTERLACING THE ROOTS: A NETWORK OF RELATIONSHIPS

Being an average housewife and mother, I had just begun to understand the word *ecology* when I met one of its robust children, *ecosystem*.

My introduction came on a soggy day one winter. I helped chaperone a sixth grade field trip to the marshy baylands at the southeastern tip of San Francisco Bay. On high platforms that jutted out into the marsh, we discovered that an ecosystem was one of nature's communities. Here each living member, plant or animal, is indispensable to the life of every other member.

"How fascinating," I remarked on the way home.

In May I accompanied a busload of fifth graders to the tidepools in the rocky cliffs on Monterey Bay. Here I found another ecosystem, where dozens of crabs scampered in and out of crystalline pools. We learned that the crabs feed on decaying animal matter from nearby marshes. They convert it into food that can be assimilated by fish that feed on the crabs and are in turn eaten by man.

113

"How beautifully planned," I remarked that evening at the dinner table.

In August our family camped for a week among the California redwoods. We saw the huge, old trees reigning over their own special ecosystem of underbrush, madrones, squirrels, and deer. In a special display area, we followed our guide, a park ranger, in the examination of a fallen redwood. Its roots were surprisingly shallow.

"Because the redwoods grow no deep taproots," the ranger explained, "they must live in groves. Their shallow, fragile roots reach out to interlace with each other. This network provides a solid foundation, and the trees literally hold each other up."

"How like a family," I remarked at our twilight campfire. "When it's a marsh, a tidepool, or a forest, they call it an *ecosystem*. But when it's a man and wife and household of children, *family* is the name."

A little firsthand observation has turned up some exciting evidences of this parallel between nature and families. We will be looking at some of these evidences in the next six chapters.

Ephesians 4:15-16 says: "But we are meant to hold firmly to the truth in love, and to grow up in every way into Christ, the head. For it is from the head that the whole body, as a harmonious structure knit together by the joints with which it is provided, grows by the proper functioning of individual parts to its full maturity in love" (Phillips). Here is one more reminder that interlacing the roots is the special technique that holds families together and makes possible our growing into strong and beautiful human ecosystems.

14

Our Wonderful Each Others

The worst part of every camping trip we have ever taken has been locating a campsite. We own one of the largest tents made, which always eliminates a number of cozy spots. Beyond that, we are all usually tired from the long trip. Most of us are willing to settle for almost whatever. But Walt (who has never been overly enthusiastic about camping out and sleeping on air mattresses anyway) holds out for the "ideal" niche in the big woods. All of this creates no little confusion and fussing. By the time the tent is finally pitched, I am wondering whether we will ever mend the family spirits sufficiently to enjoy each other's company for a week.

But invariably something happens between tent pitching and bedtime. Is it the magic of eating outdoors? The menu helps, I think. I always serve steaks and corn on the cob—knowing the rest of the week will mean canned pork and beans, powdered eggs, and lukewarm Kool-Aid. Or maybe it's the wind in the trees, a nearby stream, a vivid sunset, a Frisbee game, or a twilight hike. At any rate, by the time we gather around our first campfire, we are huddled together, wrapped in blankets, and roasting marshmallows. We sing, visit, share jokes, and make plans for the week. Then, with a warmth that wells up from deep inside me, I reaffirm my faith in a longtime creed of our family: "We've got wonderful each others!"

Family appreciation—what is it? How do we express it? Must we always say it in words? Are words enough?

Walt is one of the most considerate men alive, right down to where it touches me most—the dinner table. From the first day of our marriage, he has gone through a charming, little mealtime routine. Wiping the last crumb from his face, he says, "Thank you, dear, for the delicious dinner."

He never does this out of habit. He varies it a bit and even omits it at a meal now and then. Sometimes he tells me he thinks the food could have been better. But when he says thank you and smiles, he looks so satisfied that I cannot doubt his gratitude.

Table graces, Thanksgiving Day observances, the thank you of a store clerk at the end of a business transaction—we are all familiar with them. We trained our children to say please and not to forget thank you. This mechanical reaction to favors given them was part of their civilizing process.

But we soon realized that such habits can be as meaningless as thanking the Bell system's recorded-time lady. They suggest the fat man, Holle Bolle, whom we met in a Dutch amusement park. Built of concrete, he stood near a concession stand. By recording, he shouted: "Put your papers here."

Children scurried to tear off their candy and gum wrappers and throw them into Holle Bolle's gaping mouth. As he sucked in the trash, the funny man called out: "Thank you much. Thank you much."

Not only have our children learned the verbal courtesies of gratitude, but in their childlike manner they have led us beyond habits, forms, and mechanical reactions to see gratitude as an attitude that thrives on searching out reasons to exist. Gratitude must be expressed to survive. All their lives our children have been demonstrating for us that appreciation is the abundant overflow of a heart bursting to say, "My life is richer because of what you are and do."

They began with their first smile. Long awaited and coaxed, yet it came as a spontaneous response to that warm world of mother that held baby close and filled his tummy. This was each child's first thank you.

Ever since then, at the most unexpected moments, Martha, Tim, and Mary Jane have given vent to verbal bursts of appreciation such as:

"You make the best pancakes in the world."

"Thank you, Mom, for choosing such a good husband to be our daddy."

They have been showing us that appreciation counts the most in the little, humdrum areas of life. Under their tutelage, we are learning to express our thanks more consistently for the salt, the back rub, the carrying out of the trash. Gratitude for all these practical sorts of things is helping to build lifelong root systems between the five persons in our household and to hold the grove together.

When Tim and Walt wrestle on the living room floor or the back lawn, I am often aware that I am seeing appreciation in action. In effect, our son is saying, "Dad, I think you're terrific. I appreciate you."

When occasionally I come home from a Saturday morning shopping trip to find lunch on the table, the house picked up and vacuumed, or three loads of wash folded neatly on my bed, I suspect that my girls really do appreciate their mother. Furthermore, every time I attend a concert, a play, or a cross-country meet, or hear one of the children give a testimony in church, I feel rewarded and thanked. For each event furnishes a bit of concrete evidence that my encouragement and proddings have been successful and appreciated.

Whenever we are invited to help chaperone a field trip, or simply to go along "because I want to share Hamlet with you, Mom"; or to make a pizza for the Thespian party because "everybody loves your pizza," we feel appreciated.

Family appreciation, family unity, family cohesion—
where do they come from? we've often asked. On what basis
can we reach out to interlace the roots with appreciation
and thereby hold each other up?

After living for two decades as an adult in a family of my
own, I have concluded that roots of appreciation, unity, and
cohesion spring from mutual, loving respect.

One of the real tragedies we have observed in today's society is the trend towards fatherless families. Our children
live close to this unhappy situation at school, where a growing percentage of their friends and classmates live with single mothers. This fact was startling enough to me. But
when I heard of these children's reactions, I was horrified.

Martha told me several years ago, "Most of the girls I
know who have no fathers say they wouldn't want one anyway."

"They wouldn't want one?" I asked, taken completely
by surprise.

"That's right, Mom," she insisted. "But I know why.
It's because they've never known what a really good father
is. I'm so thankful for my daddy."

I sensed in her quick tribute to a worthy father that our
daughter appreciated her daddy because she respected him.
And not only so. She had learned this sort of respect because he also respects her. For as Martha's parents, and
Tim's and Mary Jane's as well, we are both learning that
respect is a two-way thing in healthy families.

When the children were little and we still envisioned
ourselves as the big, wise, powerful shapers of pliable little
lives, we allowed our authoritative position to rule the
household. We reached out with our shallow roots to en-
gulf the new sprouts and to hold up their sapling structures.
"Children, obey your parents," the Bible said (Ephesians
6:1). Our duty was to enforce this biblical command in

our home. We had to teach respect for authority while the saplings were still green.

I still believe this was as it should have been. But little by little, without our realizing it, we learned to respect our children as well. As they grew more independent and more competent to express themselves, we gave an increasing consideration to their needs, their wishes, their differences.

Still there have been areas where we have violated some of the rules of mutual respect in our family. Like many other families, we all enjoy teasing one another. But as so easily happens when we indulge in the matching of witticisms, our teasing sometimes gets out of hand. In the free flow of words, all spoken in good nature and with mutual understanding that nothing is serious, we have often joshed each other unwisely.

All seems to go well, until one of the children retaliates by calling Mom or Dad by an uncomplimentary title such as "crazy" or "stupid." This action signals the end of the game. Now we must become serious, for to call Dad "crazy" is to show disrespect.

When this first happened, we wondered where we had failed in communicating respect for authority. Then one day, the children answered our question.

"But Mom, you call us by the same kinds of names," the children defended.

We hastened to justify our actions with the lame excuse, "That's different."

"What's so different about it?" they wanted to know.

How could we say that we could treat them as we liked because we were parents, and they had to respect us, but that they may not treat us as they liked, because they were only children?

We couldn't!

Instead, we had to admit—out loud to the whole offended

family—that we had been wrong. We remembered now that not only did Ephesians 6:1-2 command children to obey their parents, but Ephesians 6:4 added, "Fathers, do not provoke your children to anger." We realized that this applied to the kind of unfair "privilege" we were taking.

Our sudden confrontation with logic revealed to us a great truth we need to grasp in our attempt to interlace the family roots, namely: a family is a place where each member deserves respect as a person. We parents are not to demand this respect because of who we are. We may however earn our children's esteem through extending the same sort of courtesy to them that we show to each other.

The whole idea reminded me of 1 Peter 5:5, a verse I had known for years: "Ye younger, submit yourselves unto the elder. Yea, all of you be subject one to another, and be clothed with humility" (KJV).

We began to apply this principle to many areas of family relationships and found it to be extremely practical. If one of the children, without permission, burst through our closed bedroom door, we felt justified in reprimanding him. By fair exchange of respect, we had to learn to honor each child's right to privacy and never to storm uninvited through his closed door. While we expect apologies from a child who disobeys or hurts us, we must also freely apologize and make restitution for our wrongdoings. We resent being laughed at for our stupidities. Hence, we must never laugh at one of our children in his weak moments. We reserve for ourselves the right to opinions that differ from the rest of the family's, to fit our important activities into the family schedule, to ask for understanding when we fail in dozens of ways. At last we are seeing how impossible it would be to hold a family together unless we extend these same rights to our children.

There are times for us as parents to demand full explanations, blind obedience, and other forms of submission to parental authority—but never without giving full respect to the value of the other person.

One of the most difficult concepts for us to grasp was the role of privacy in the development of family appreciation and togetherness. This should have come easily to me, for I am a private person. I need some periods of silent aloneness each day. Often in the early mothering years I had to fight to snatch even a few minutes for quiet meditation. I recall rising daily at 5:00 A.M., sneaking as soundlessly as possible down the huge Dutch stairway to a dark, empty living room, so I could find a few moments alone with God before my day went into a whirl—only to be followed shortly by a sleepy, pajama-clad son, ready for attention and the day's action. Eagerly I awaited the day when all three children would go to school. Since it finally came, I have thoroughly enjoyed the freedom offered to me by the many hours of delicious solitude.

However, when Martha announced one summer that she wanted to stay home alone while the family went camping, I recoiled. Leave her alone? Mercy, no! Not only did I fear the idea, I felt certain her request indicated that we were not important to her anymore. Surely the family roots were becoming disentangled.

"But, Mother," our frustrated teenager wailed, "you want to be alone sometimes, too. And you are—all day, every day—while we're at school. Can't you let me have a chance too?"

Once more, a daughter's logic lessened my fears and helped an overly conscientious mother to make the break with one more hang-up. We made arrangements for Martha to spend the vacation at home. She went to summer school in the mornings, passed her afternoons in coveted solitude, and entertained her grandmothers as nightly sleeping guests.

What did this experiment do to the solidarity of our

family? Absence and time for personal reflection actually strengthened the bonds between us. Next vacation, we were all ready to go *together,* and had a heightened capacity for enjoyment of that togetherness. Furthermore, the experience taught us a new appreciation and respect for each other's persons, privacy, and wonderful each otherness.

> Time out for a thank-you.
> Thank You God, for families.

So wrote Jerry Vajda in one of the most beautiful pieces of free verse about families that I have ever read.

> Universal as bread, water, air,
> Indispensable as life—
> This gift it required a God to prepare,
> This nest, this bond, this shelter—
> A family.
>
> Someone to grow with, someone to love,
> Someone to love you, someone to know,
> Flesh of your flesh, bone of your bone,
> Someone to laugh with, someone to miss,
> Someone to wait for, someone to cry over,
> Someone . . . a cluster of someones
> Tied warmly together for love.*

J. J. VAJDA

*From "God Makes Us a Family" by J. Vajda, © 1966.

15

Thank God for Grandparents

Of all the wonderful each others in a family circle, among the choicest are the grandparents. I confess I have not always appreciated this.

I grew up surrounded by grandparents. As a child, I recall frequent train rides to the big city to visit mother's parents in their suburban cottage overlooking a tiny lake. We always spent Christmas with a huge crowd of cousins, aunts, and uncles at my paternal grandparents' farm. Because I had never known anything else, I found it difficult to imagine a world without grandmothers to churn butter and entertain us with a squatty button-jar, or grandfathers to take us fishing or let us help milk the cows. Because they were always a part of my life, I took them for granted and never stopped to consider what riches they brought to me over the years.

In fact, when Walt and I were married, we pinned our dreams on an exciting military career that would take us around the world—a career that would give us the opportunity to test out life away from the influence of grandparents. And to give our children a chance to do the same.

But the Lord had other designs, at least to begin with. Walt's first assignment kept him stationed twenty miles from home for four years. During this time, Martha and Tim were born. Then, just as we began to see that living near grandparents had a few advantages, things started to change.

Two weeks before Mary Jane arrived, Walt left for Mississippi for three months of school. He planned to return home in May, help us pack up our things, and take us with him to Europe.

Instead, one day before Mary Jane and I came home from the hospital, Mother's realtor sold her house, where we were living. The new owner gave me thirty days to vacate. Once again, our plans were changed, and I was given one more opportunity to see the greatness of the extended family that takes in grandparents.

Four weeks of hectic planning and packing followed. On Walt's and my fourth wedding anniversary, Grandma Herr and Great-Grandma accompanied our little family to Los Angeles on the train. Here they helped me transfer luggage, baby, toddlers, and a two-day's supply of diapers and food onto the cross-country streamliner that carried us to our daddy in the Deep South.

I suspected only mildly that we would miss those lovely people left behind. That the children would miss them I hardly considered. Of course we expected the grandparents to feel deprived. Grandparents were supposed to be sentimental. As for us, we welcomed the freedom we had so long dreamed of.

However, the flow of letters from home over the next years helped to build in me an increasing appreciation for the role of grandparents in the growing up of the family. While we lived in Holland, Mother wrote often of our two Mary Janes—one, the little rosebud bundle she had last held and kissed on a windy, railway platform; the other, that blonde "Dutch" girl whose photographs we kept sending, trying to "make me believe she's the same Mary Jane you took away from me."

Grandma Herr and Great-Grandma wrote about Timmie nearly running his chubby legs off in the Los Angeles terminal as he tried to catch the New Orleans Pullman special.

We detected something deeper than sentimentality in the nostalgic letters and the tape recorded visits that we shuttled back and forth across a continent and an ocean. One tape especially became an instant favorite with our whole family. It featured Great-Grandma's seventy-seven-year-old voice singing, with unbelievable clarity and stability,

> High in the treetops' leafy boughs,
> The birdies are building their nests.
> 'Twas God the Father taught them how
> To build, every birdie, his best.
>
> AUTHOR UNKNOWN

I recognized the song as one she had taught me when I was little. I even let myself feel a bit sentimental as this simple recording carried me back into a childhood rich with memories of grandparents loving me, teaching me, sharing hundreds of good times with me, helping me to build some strong, healthy roots.

I didn't dare admit how much I was beginning to miss the dear folks at home. But I wrote them weekly to share the cute talk and charming antics of three grandchildren, who were growing up without the benefits of nearby grandparents.

When we returned to the States, we visited home as frequently as time and funds would allow. We determined somehow to make up for lost time and do all we could to foster a growing relationship between the generations. But when Walt received orders for an isolated tour of duty in Southeast Asia, I balked at the idea of spending the year at home near "Mama." All these years, I had been nurturing my independence. Not anxious to lose it once more, I wanted to keep a bit of distance between us.

I honestly can't recall what changed my mind and finally made me willing to settle in Hometown, USA. I suspect that the "effectual fervent prayer" of four loving, lonesome grandparents in central California had something to do with it. What I do recall with clarity, however, are the special learning experiences that year held for me—experiences in striking the balance between independence and reliance.

When we had been newlyweds, still living under our mothers' watchful eyes, Walt and I had had only a hazy understanding of the place of grandparents in the family. We knew well the scriptural command "Honor your father and your mother" (Exodus 20:12). Yet, because we were anxious to keep them from intruding, we did not know what to do with them.

But with Walt half a world away, I soon found how valuable grandparents, mothers, even in-laws could be when I needed encouragement, advice, and adult companionship. I was surprised to see how alike my mother and I had grown through our years of separate living—years in which we had gained an independence that was leading us to maturity and mutual appreciation.

Most important of all, I learned that children not only enjoy their grandparents, they need them. In fact, I have almost decided it would be better for parents to adopt some lonely older folks as substitute grandparents for their children than to let them grow up without grandparental relationships.

By the time Walt left the service, we were actually ready to go home and settle down close to the grandparents. Today, we are both thanking God for the presence of those deep, mature, grandparental roots in the family grove. We have come to regard them as an integral part of the family and not as outdated, potential interferers to be held at a safe distance.

In a fascinating study of Bible families, I have observed that this is an ancient attitude approved by God. One verse in Leviticus especially impressed me: "You shall rise up before the grayheaded, and honor the aged, and you shall revere your God" (Leviticus 19:32). Honoring the elderly and revering God rank very close to each other in His eyes.

This extended family concept doesn't mean we all move in together under one long roof, as is the practice in some societies. To us it means a simple reaching out to share both happy times and sad ones, fun times and serious ones, active times and quiet ones, work and play, achievements and failures.

We began to grasp this broader sense of family while Walt was overseas. The children and I gathered each Friday night at Grandma and Grandpa Herr's for TV with ice cream and cookies. Since then, the children have practiced the idea of sharing with extended family by giving up a bed and sleeping on the couch whenever a grandparent or two comes for a visit.

Today, whenever one of the high schoolers performs in a play, a concert, or a cross-country final, of course the grandparents are invited. And they usually attend—even ninety-year-old Great-Grandma. Our teenagers reciprocate when they stop by the organ after a Sunday morning service to say "hi" to the organist, Grandma Alice.

We act out the extended family when we plan a trip to the beach or a visit with friends, and, because Grandma Herr lives with us, we don't have to convene a family council to decide whether she should be invited. She's part of the family.

This has become possible only as we have reserved some special times without grandparents. A second honeymoon or just an evening out for Mom and Dad alone; parent and child outings with individual children; occasions for Mom and Dad and all the kids to do something together—all are needed to nourish growth of the independent family unit as well as all the one-to-one relationships.

We arrived at this viewpoint gradually. As our immediate family gained independent strength and maturity, we felt less threatened by the older generation and more appreciative of what they had to offer. As our children grew older, we came to feel more at home with intergenerational communication. So, when my mother retired from her Mexican mission work, we were ready to invite her to move her mobile home to our new hometown. At last, we could welcome her to be a part of our church and to share on a continuing basis our community and our children's school activities.

In so doing we became aware of an increasing number of functions performed by grandparents in the family unit. They had begun by passing on genetically many special gifts to their grandchildren. We have discovered a bonus is given to both generations when these same grandparents live close enough to share in the development of these talents. Nothing thrills me more than to watch Mary Jane and Grandma Herr sitting side by side on the couch while busily filling their sketch pads; or Martha and Grandma Alice playing a piano duet; or Tim and Grandpa Bill tinkering in Grandpa's bicycle shop. Through these choice experiences, I sense that the children are strengthening their ties with the past, interlacing their growing roots with the deeper, sturdier roots in the family grove.

Grandparents can also help to teach respect for differences in opinions, interests, and tastes. We are seeing this more clearly these days since Grandma Herr has come to live with us.

When she first came, our children went on living just as they always had—playing their music, wearing their own styles of clothes, planning their schedules. Before long, they discovered that Grandma sometimes had different ideas about these things. We never saw any serious confrontations. But the children came to see that their grandmother has a point of view worth listening to and respecting. The beauty of it is that they all seem, now, to know their boundaries pretty well. Because the children want to see Grandma happy, they are willing to change a few things here and there. Grandma, at the same time, does not question their life-styles. Together, we are growing in our awareness that in a family we have to stay flexible and make room for each individual to grow his own personal roots. For the only roots that hold up the grove are those that maintain their identity and separateness as they intertwine.

One of the truly lovely things we have watched in our children's lives is their obvious appreciation for their grandparents. Martha told me recently, "Mom, I sometimes hear you talking downstairs and think you're Grandma Alice. I dash down because I want to see Grandma, and then find it's only you."

We both laughed at the unintended implication. I was pleased to see a teenager who could get excited about the coming of a grandmother whom she sees several times every week of her life.

I remember the day when Grandma stood in the kitchen as Tim came through. He stopped, put his hand on her shoulder, and said with gusto: "Viva la Grandma!"

I remember that at the death of my paternal grandfather, whom our children hardly knew, Tim said, "Boy, am I glad we went to see Grandma and Grandpa last spring!"

More than anything, my children have opened my eyes to see how terribly special grandparents are. They have prepared me to reach out and draw these dear ones as full-fledged members into the circle of our wonderful each others. This was brought home to me forcibly one evening as Mother and I washed dishes together at my sink.

That morning, I had visited a friend whose lovely home had four bedrooms, a large family room, and a dining room. As I returned to my little three-bedroom house with its tiny living room and family kitchen, my attitude was tinged by a shamefully large dose of jealousy. After all, I reasoned, what do my friend, her husband, and their one small son need with all that space, while our family with three teenagers squeezes into this little cracker box?

With my hands in the soapsuds that night, I told my mother about my friend's "mansion." I opened my mouth to complain about the unfairness of it all. Interrupting, Mother urged me to look across the cluttered breakfast bar to see what was going on at our dining table. What I saw convinced me I had been looking at things from a distorted viewpoint. There, seated at the table, all three of my children were playing a lively game with their great-grandmother.

"You know, Mother," I said with new conviction as I returned to the dishes, "it isn't fair. Judie has that big, beautiful house but only one child to brighten her life. And she hasn't a relative living within fifteen-hundred miles. Her poor little boy hardly even knows his grandparents. At the same time, my kids have more nearby grandparents than they know what to do with."

Then, scooping up a handful of silverware from the rinse water and placing it carefully in the dish drainer, I announced, "We've got the richest family alive. We're just running over with beautiful grandparents—the wonderfulest each others on earth."

16

Listening Makes Parents Great

Why the old VW squareback always chose the hottest, smoggiest days of the year to act up, I never fully understood. Unless it hated the combination of smog, heat, and traffic as I did. At any rate, I recall with choking poignancy a few instances when I was tempted to park the reluctant vehicle and walk home. One of these occasions was the spring afternoon I took the children to the orthodontist.

The car had not been performing up to its potential for some time. So, lacking the power needed to handle dangerous freeway entrances and exits, I had taken to San Tomas Expressway. This meant eighteen long miles of stop-and-go, heavy, pre-rush hour traffic one way followed by eighteen miles of stop-and-go, bumper-to-bumper, rush hour traffic home again.

Our long-legged teenagers sat scrunched into the tiny car. And to think, when we first bought it to replace the "bug," ten years earlier, we had thought it quite spacious. As we inched our way homeward, we almost smothered in the heat and smog that poured through our open windows and seeped in through every crack. To complicate matters, the car's feeble engine stalled at every other light along the way. Four raw tempers rubbed each other and ignited into ugly little bursts of peevish disposition. Sitting at the wheel, I fussed and fumed at the lights, the heat, the smog, the kids—resenting the mother lot that had turned me into a chauffeur.

*Why must I waste so much of my life behind the wheel
of this stubborn, little, undersized automobile, carting a
bunch of grouchy teenagers all over the Santa Clara Valley?*
I stormed inside.

That evening, after the sun had set and cool, bay breezes
were blowing through our house, I continued to complain.
For weeks now, I had been wrestling with increasingly frequent intrusions into my important work schedule and un-
realistic demands on my already low supply of nervous energy. I had fought the problem, resented it, struggled to
eliminate it. In spite of my vigorous efforts, I was apparently stuck with the situation.

That night, Walt promised to take another look at the
VW engine, which always seemed to perform so well for
him. Beyond this, he simply reminded me that chauffeur-
ing was one of my mothering duties.

As I chafed and grumbled to the Lord once more, I realized that Walt was right. This was my duty. And if it
was my duty, then perhaps I could find a way to perform
it without allowing each trip to shatter my nerves and the
kids' dispositions. I had been lamenting the unpleasant
fact that these trips robbed me of time I needed to relax and
listen to my children. Now, once I had accepted the inev-
itability of the situation and begun to look at it with cool
logic, I saw something embarrassingly obvious.

These nasty run-about trips could actually become the
very schedule spots I was looking for. For, shut up together
in the car for sometimes a half hour or more at a time, we
had the ideal setup for visiting and getting acquainted.

My discovery excited me so, I could hardly wait for the
next appointment to try it out. In a few days, I had my
opportunity. The difference was astounding. Once I was
willing to change my attitude and turn to listening, the
whole atmosphere brightened—even before the VW was repaired. Today, instead of dreading these trips, I find I can

actually anticipate each scheduled opportunity to listen and get close to the fascinating teenagers who share their lives with me.

By nature I am a talker, not a listener. Since Walt is a quiet person, his silence encourages me to talk on. But not so with the children. From the beginning, they demanded an ear. At times this was difficult to give, especially when they prattled at such a trivial level. At other times I found listening to be sheer delight.

I discovered this record in one of my letters from Holland to home. It speaks of my daily custom of doing lunch "jishes" with three-year-old Martha while Tim and Mary Jane napped:

> A time I feel increasingly important, this Mommy-daughter hour each day. We talk about all kinds of things, from Dutch vocabulary to what (besides Baby Magic) makes our hands beautiful. Then she gladly tramps up the stairs in stocking feet, laughs at Tim's loud snoring, and scrambles into bed.

During those years, I learned to tune my ears to the little gems of wisdom our three toddlers shared. Without realizing it, I was opening the door of my own heart and mind to their unique, developing personalities. I was getting acquainted with my children.

But I was only beginning to learn the importance and the techniques of effective listening that would result in growth of strong family roots. As the children grew through our interactions at the daily level, I soon discovered that listening is a complex thing, an art to be worked at and perfected throughout the growing process.

To begin with, I found that listening involves respecting one another's will to share. For good reasons, my mother had told me I must never keep a secret from her. The only promise I was free to break, was one to "not tell my mother."

While, as I grew up, I did actually keep many secrets, yet when my turn came to be mother, I began teaching my children to tell me everything. It was the only safe way to go.

However, we had to learn that secret keeping and sharing with others outside the family was sometimes normal and healthy. When Walt's nephew visited with us, he confided some of his problems to us. Later we told his mother about the visit.

"That's great," she responded. "I'm sure he told you things he couldn't share with me."

I raised an eyebrow and wondered how she could accept with such pleasure her son's departure from exclusive confidence in her. Then the day came when Martha told me she had taken some of her problems elsewhere, without sharing them first with me. I was tempted to fret, until I remembered my sister-in-law's words. Did this mean I need not fear the loss of a daughter's confidence just because she kept a few secrets from me?

Paul Tournier, the great Swiss physician, further put me at ease about allowing children to keep secrets. In his small book titled simply *Secrets*, he says: "Every human being needs secrecy in order to become himself and no longer only a member of his tribe. . . . Every man, to feel respected as an individual, needs to feel absolutely free to say what he wishes and to keep as a secret what he wishes."[1]

Dr. Tournier does not suggest that parents should never pry important facts and admissions out of their children. But he does urge us to exercise caution and discernment in all intrusions into the secret lives of our growing children.

My daughters have begun teaching me another vital lesson about listening. They have helped me realize that they often share with me for the joy or relief of sharing and not always as a request for advice. Martha has always been an open kind of person who shares her inner self readily. We have spent many hours walking, riding, sitting on the edge of one another's beds, sharing ideas, burdens, dreams, and problems. Being the mother-counselor, I have always tried to come up with some solid solutions to her problems. How shocking to discover that my answers were often too pat to be workable!

I first realized this when I found that session after session we were reviewing the same old problems. Certain basic problems kept reappearing at each new stage of her development. One night, when we had been over the familiar area for the hundredth time, I began a routine answer. Martha interrupted me. "Mom, I know what you're going to say. And it doesn't work."

"Then I guess you'll have to find your own answer," I said in desperation. As I spoke the words, I realized that what this girl had needed all these years was not my neatly packaged answers. She had needed my sympathetic ear and my willingness to pray and let her struggle with her own problems in her own way.

Mary Jane, on the other hand, is much more of a keep-it-all-to-herself-er. When she shared a burden, I found myself trying to cheer her up by offering alternative explanations to disturbing happenings. She always rejected my efforts, and I wondered why, until the day she found both the words and the courage to tell me, "Mom, I don't want any advice. That's why I don't tell you very much. I just want you to listen to me."

How easily I had been giving advice, squelching the joy of sharing, hindering spontaneity, and destroying that eagerness to share. My girls have been helping me decide that we have to earn the right to be our children's audience by being content to be just that—a sympathetic audience.

I keep asking, how can I decide when I'm supposed to offer advice and when my listening ear is all that's needed? That's a tough one. But I am beginning to see that the answer involves listening with ears, eyes, heart, and my total being—being sensitive to the whole person who is sharing himself with me. Further, it means listening to the voice of the Holy Spirit. Over and over I go back to James 1:5 and claim that special promise: "If any of you lacks wisdom, let him ask of God, who gives to all men generously and without reproach, and it will be given to him." I never seem to find it easy to strike the necessary balance. But I can testify that it is possible.

When Martha was fifteen, she came to us with a difficult request. She wanted our permission to dance with her friends at Thespian and choral parties. Because we had been taught that dancing was a dangerous sin, and had been forbidden to participate in such activities when we were young, we automatically labeled dancing off-limits to our own children. As they grew older and could understand our objections, we had explained how we felt. However, not anxious to arouse their curiosity and undue interest, we had never made a big issue of it.

For years we had known Martha would one day challenge us on this point, for no child was ever more endowed with a sense of rhythm or responsiveness to music. From the time she could stand in her playpen, she had bounced to the sound of music whenever and wherever she heard it.

Now, shyly at first, then with increasing boldness, she confessed her interest. "When can I stop living by my parents' convictions which I don't share, and decide this thing for myself?" she asked.

How could we listen to this one? We did not have to; we could easily draw a clear line and make her stay behind it. After all, that was our right as parents—maybe even our duty.

But somehow, this idea made both Walt and me more uneasy than ever. We recalled stories of young people in our day whose parents had boasted, "My Mary never attends dances," while the whole community knew she had been sneaking out to do the very thing her parents insisted she was not doing.

No, we decided, our daughter had the right to be heard—to bring her ideas out in the open. At least we must let her explain her reasons and plead her case.

"When we feel you're ready to make a wise decision, we'll consider it," we told her.

"You mean, when I'm ready to decide it your way!" she shot back defensively.

"No," we countered. "If you've evaluated this thing in prayer and can show us that you've reasoned it out and are prepared to take responsibility for your actions, then we'll give you your freedom."

With a sigh of relief, she went on to present her reasons. She assured us that she understood our objections. But she had prayed much about it, discussed it with Christian friends and youth leaders, and before God she felt perfectly right about the thing. Then with tender concern in her eyes, she told us, "I know this is a hard thing for you. You've always felt so strongly about the subject, and I know changes are hard to accept."

As we listened that day in a new way and gave our daughter a freedom we had never wanted to give her, we learned that listening does not always mean approving our children's decisions. But it does involve sensing when they are mature enough to handle certain kinds of decisions on their own and take responsibility for their own actions.

Listening has proved to be hard work. The older our children grow, the more our role as parents has become primarily a counseling role. We are learning that this means being prepared to listen not only when our clocks say, This is the listening moment. We must be ready to listen whenever, as often, and as long as our young charges feel the need to share with us.

During a particularly difficult experience in her high

school life, Martha spent many long hours keeping me up to date on the latest developments. Her frustrations mounted. I advised her how to free herself from the sticky relationship. From my adult vantage point, it looked so easy. I was realistic enough to know this was hardly so for her. Yet, when she returned again and again with the same old problem, I was often tempted to cut her off and tell her not to come back until she had done what I suggested. I especially felt this way late one Saturday night. She perched on the edge of my bed. As she poured out all the old, familiar lines, I fought both sleep and the urge to send the young night-owl off to bed so we could both spend our time profitably. When at last she left me alone with my dreams, I felt more frustrated and useless than ever.

The next evening, during a testimony time at church, Martha stood and paid a public tribute to her mother. "She's the greatest mother a girl could ever have," she told the congregation. "She's always willing to listen when I need to talk."

So that's what makes a mother great in the eyes of her daughter? I thought. Somewhere inside I felt I did not deserve this kind of tribute. Not I, the mother who always talked too much and listened too little—who had begun motherhood well equipped with answers, doctrines, sage advice, and a ready tongue to dispense all three.

Yet, in a beautiful moment of honest reflection, I realized that I had also begun my parental vocation with a deep sense of compassion. Perhaps through this channel, my three little ones had found a way to entwine their tender roots with mine. With the pressure of growing love, they had managed to teach me that my most important mission was no longer to share all my wisdom but to listen.

17

Shut the Door—Gezellig!

Personal privacy—how I love it! Not until I studied Dutch, however, did I find a word that adequately describes how my moments of seclusion make me feel. *Gezellig*, like many foreign words, cannot be translated by a single English word. Instead, it wraps up warmth, coziness, delight, and security into a neat, little bundle of eight letters.

Living in Holland with a family of toddlers also taught us that family privacy, too, is *gezellig*. During that first memorable winter in the Netherlands, we had so much privacy that it turned into isolation. As we overreacted to the pain of that solitude, however, we began to distinguish the fine line that separates isolation from its cousin, privacy.

The old brick house we called home for our first two years abroad rose up three floors and spread over a tiny, earth-walled cellar. Located in the picturesque village of Baarn, the drafty place was as big as its city address implied. The living-dining room alone was big enough to accommodate a Sunday morning congregation.

"All this house for the five of us?" I asked, when my husband first showed it to me.

We climbed two long flights of stairs to the second floor, where we found three huge bedrooms. Another flight led us to two more rooms, tucked up under the eaves.

"It looks as if we've rented a boardinghouse," Walt suggested.

Boardinghouse indeed. Immediately my mind went to work searching out ways to use all this rambling space—Bible classes, social events, youth rallies, women's coffees. Mentally I transformed the onetime baron's mansion into a buzzing mission station.

In reality, though, we passed the first six months huddled around a coal-burning monster in the corner of the living room. Visitors consisted of the milkman, the bread boy, the plumber, and an assortment of bill collectors looking for a former tenant.

By spring, we were desperate for company. Throwing open the doors, we welcomed, along with the rare moments of sunshine, every human being who would come.

And come they did: a Stateside acquaintance in May, a traveling evangelist from Athens in June, a live-in Dutch maid in August. For the next three years our house vibrated with activity. A growing variety of people used it for meetings, retreats, hobbies, socializing, and hotel services.

One day, during an interlude in the hubbub, we sat down to a rare meal *alone*—the first in months.

Martha picked at her food and asked, "Where's Gerry?"

Tim played with his spoon and added, "Where's Chrys?"

In the high chair Mary Jane jabbered a monologue over her food. Her voice echoed around the empty kitchen with the fifteen-foot ceiling. Walt and I stared at each other like strangers.

That was when we recalled the advice of our Dutch friend Brum, who had helped us locate this house. When we first moved in, we shared with him our dreams about making it useful.

He cautioned, "Beware! Don't let too many house guests crowd out your family privacy."

We snickered a bit at his idea, then. After all, Brum was a conservative Dutchman who had no children and an apartment too small to entertain crowds, even if he wanted to. What could he know about the American family pattern?

But now, eating together in awkward, unaccustomed silence, we began to understand what too many house guests were doing to our family unity. No longer did we laugh at Brum's ideas. And in the years since then, we have concluded that he was absolutely right.

In order to develop properly and reach the goal of family unit maturity, every family must jealously guard ample time alone.

But do we dare to isolate ourselves as a family? we wondered. We do live in communities, where each home contributes something to the lives of all the others. Surely there must be a way to learn our limits of involvement and to function as effective community members while keeping the family unity intact.

On a field trip to the seashore tidepools, Mary Jane and I discovered an ecosystem family that spoke to the question of this balanced kind of relationship. On a wide strip of sandy beach, we observed the meeting of two large, natural communities, or families—the ocean and the tidepools.

Here, Mary Jane's teacher told us, creatures from both natural communities mingle to help each other. We learned, though, that each family respects certain boundaries. Large, seagoing fish could never exist in the shallow tidepools. Yet they feed on small animals and decaying vegetable matter swept out to them from those tidepools by retreating tides. Barnacles fastened to the rocky ledge of shoreline would quickly flounder if they rushed out with the first wave that washed over them. But they depend on food carried in from ocean depths by those same threatening breakers.

As I watched and learned about the ecosystem, I marveled at the great wisdom God has exemplified in nature for us. Unlike the many creatures in these well-ordered,

natural communities, we human families can so easily fail
to understand our place in the community and may retreat
from other families with the turn of the tides.

From the communities where we live, a myriad of
influences seek admittance to our homes. Some knock
persistently on our doors. Others creep in through un-
guarded windows. Some are beneficial; others, deadly.
Still others, neither good nor bad in themselves, bring
potential both for blessing and catastrophe. Deciding which
category each fits demands a superhuman blend of sensitivity, discipline, watchfulness, and clear sense of family
mission. We find ourselves constantly facing such questions as:

Shall we banish the TV set to the Goodwill box, or
shall we teach the children to control it? When does
church involvement become too much, so we risk losing
our children while attempting to win the world? How
shall we adapt to those trying times when Dad has to work
long overtime-hour days, to minimize the strain such a
grueling temporary experience puts on family growth?
Is it possible to take in too many concerts and museums?
Picnics and beach trips? School activities? How important
is individual privacy of each family member? Are we
being selfish when we leave the children with Grandma
and take a second honeymoon? Is it ever right to force a
child to choose between a week at camp (or visiting
cousins) and going on the annual family camping trip?

We find that how we deal with these kinds of challenges
teaches our children more about values and priorities than
hours of theoretical instruction administered in private
closets. This is particularly true in matters of hospitality.
Such family experiences foster an awareness of community responsibility and develop skills for fulfilling that
responsibility.

At our wedding, Walt and I sang by recording a song written for the occasion by my mother. One line went, "We pray that to our fireside, each friend and guest invited may learn from us of Jesus."

Repeatedly since then, our home has served as a refuge for outsiders who, it is to be hoped, learn "from us of Jesus." Our children began life in an atmosphere of constant involvement with others and their needs. Throughout the years, they have watched our home serve in a variety of ways as a center of Christian ministry. They, too, have taken part in many of these activities. Perhaps most important of all, as persons and as a family, we have let our door stand open so friends, relatives, and neighbors could drop in occasionally for a meal or an evening together—thus taking part, for a time, in the life of our family, where love and togetherness are hard at work cementing persons into a unified structure.

Important as this outreach ministry of the family is, we are learning that outreach is not the primary function of the home in society. First of all, the family is a nursery for development of human resources. Here character is formed, values are set, and patterns of life and personal relationships are established. We discovered the hard way that, in practical terms, this means wherever service to outsiders conflicts with this essential character molding function, *the family must come first.*

We had this forcibly brought to our attention through Chrys, a traveling evangelist from Greece. He was one of the most beneficial outside influences ever to enter our family. He made our home his headquarters whenever he was in Holland. He was a young bachelor who valued his privacy and respected ours as well. However, we had our difficult times.

I remember especially the last spring he stayed with us. He was compiling a commentary on the book of Ephesians.

Up in his third-floor attic room, he spent each morning poring over theological books. At noon, he joined the children and me for lunch. He longed to share his stimulating discoveries with someone, and I was handy.

So, day after day, Chrys turned our lunch hour into a deep theological discussion. First he aired the various viewpoints he had studied on a given passage. Then he asked me, "What do you think about this, Ethel?"

All the while, my three preschoolers demanded normal mealtime attention.

"Mommy, I need some butter."

"Timmie took my fork."

"Janie spilled her milk!"

By lunch's end each day, I nearly collapsed. I was exhausted from trying to play a triple role—mother, hostess, and theological consultant. Obviously I qualified least for the last of these three.

After two or three weeks of this, Walt came to my rescue. Explaining my predicament to the eager young scholar, he requested him to refrain from theological interrogation at lunch.

"If you can save your scholarly goodies until the kids are bedded down at night," my understanding husband added, "I'd love to join the fun."

Our top priority in family privacy must go to the development of secure, purposeful adults. If we do not prepare these to go out and function redemptively in a chaotic world, who will? We have decided that turning out mature Christian teachers, doctors, homemakers, pilots, cooks, engineers, and common laborers, as well as ministers and Christian education directors, is the first duty of the home.

I think Jesus' commission to His disciples, "Go ye into all the world, and preach the gospel to every creature" (Mark 16:15, KJV), was also directed to parents. For I am sure when He spoke those words, Jesus envisioned future generations of believers infiltrating with godly character and effective witnessing the worlds of business, medicine, education, art, and politics. The nurturing of this kind of character growth involves large amounts of unhindered, unrushed, creative family privacy.

As we have worked to build strong relationships within our family circle, we have seen a strengthening of each member's ability to resist many harmful community influences that press for admittance into our home and individual lives.

Tim and Walt enjoy especially strong ties. Almost before the little fellow could say his own name, he was crawling after daddy under the family car. This choice relationship has deepened over the years.

Several years ago, Walt's returning to school in the evenings left him very little time to spend with the family. At first I wondered how the bonds would hold. Tim was entering those precarious teen years. His world held so much enticement to things of dubious worth.

But I need not have worried. The rapport between this father and son survived lustily in spite of the pressures of absence. Through those difficult years, we learned that the quantity of family privacy is not half so important as the quality. Every minute Tim and Walt were together, they spent busily sharing one another's lives.

Tim would sit on the couch beside his dad and watch him do his homework. Then they studied photography and went out on picture-shooting trips—sharing assignments and adventures, continuing to interlace the strong roots in new ways.

Throughout the years I have gained a great many new insights into this vital matter of privacy. An awareness of the need for individual privacy within the home has come slow-

ly, even painfully, however. Except for the last three years
in Holland, we have always lived in a three-bedroom house.
This means that the girls have always shared a room. And
they have always begged for a four-bedroom house "so we
can each have our own room."

"Why do you need separate rooms?" I countered every
time. I refused to take their request seriously. Most of my
life I had shared a bedroom with either my brother, some
Mexican girls we were ministering to, my mother, or a college roommate. I could remember only one short period
of about two years when I had a room to myself. I knew
Walt, in a family of eight children, had shared his room
with others. Pushing my logic back into the history books,
I recalled that whole pioneer families had shared a single
bedroom. On and on my reasoning ran, usually concluding
with, Just what makes the children of this generation so
different that they think they need private rooms?

Then when we learned that Mom Herr was coming to
live with us, it was obvious we must add at least one more
room to our tiny house. The question came up again. "We
still need separate rooms," wailed our two full-grown girls
from their cubicle at the end of the hall. As we investigated
house-planning ideas, we discovered that our only answer
was to add a partial second story. We could make it into
either two large rooms or three small ones. Guess how the
kids voted.

We drew the plans and hired the contractor. Still I could
not quite understand the rightness of it all. "But, Mom,"
Martha tried again to explain. "I need someplace I can call
my own—where I can get away and be alone."

Slowly the light came on. I recalled something Paul
Tournier had said in *Secrets*. He lamented our modern
world where we no longer have enough living space and
where persons have no corners they can call their own.[1] I

remembered, too, that while as a girl I had rarely had a room to myself, I did find countless other hiding places for protecting my secrets: the cow pasture, the small-town streets where I rode my bicycle at will and in safety, the village park, or my favorite lakeside nook beneath a willow tree. None of these special options are open to my children today. From the time they awaken in the morning until they retire at night, they are part of a busy, bustling, noisy world where the only private place to hide in safety is their own bedroom.

Today our house has five bedrooms, three bathrooms, and a study. And I do not feel extravagant about it. Instead, I think I am beginning to understand what privacy is, and how we can use it as individuals and as a family unit. As never before, I believe it can best be described with that cozy Dutch word, *gezellig!*

SUGGESTED READING

Tournier, Paul. *Secrets*. Richmond, Va.: Knox, 1963.

In easy-to-read language, Dr. Tournier examines the nature and psychological value of secrets. He traces a child's development, from the total-dependence stage of sharing every secret with parents, through the discovery of secrets and adolescence into mature adulthood. He gives some particularly valuable advice on relating to children and helping them through the various stages of total sharing, keeping secrets, and mature selective sharing. A powerful book on an intensely practical topic, vital to family and personal growth.

18

Growing Up in Him—Together

"Time for Bible study," I announced to my fourth, fifth, and seventh graders on a quiet Tuesday night. "Bring your pencils and Bibles, and let's get started."

Silence followed.

I repeated the summons and busied myself laying out maps, pictures, and study questions on the dining room table. After yet another prodding call on my part, three children straggled to their places at the table. As I handed each of them a brightly colored notebook, I detected an air of something less than enthusiasm. Throughout the study, my reluctant students wiggled in their chairs, shuffled their feet on the vinyl floor, yawned, and were generally apathetic.

About halfway through our worksheet project, Martha spoke up. Lifting her eyes only slightly from the map of the Sinai Peninsula she had been dawdling over, she ventured cautiously, "Mom, do we have to do these Bible studies anymore?"

"Wh-what do you mean—'do we *have* to?'" I stumbled over the sentence in disbelief.

"We know all these stories already," Tim offered.

"I'm sure you do," I replied, feeling grateful that at least some things had soaked in. "But this study is different. We're learning about the Bible as a whole to see how the stories fit with each other. It's something like putting the pieces of a puzzle together so we get the big picture."

"But it's boring, Mom," Mary Jane countered.

Now in a state of total shock, I wondered, Why the sudden rebellion? Hadn't Walt and I taught these children by precept and example to love and want to study the Bible?

Even before we became parents, we had read in Deuteronomy 6:6-9: "These words . . . you shall teach . . . diligently to your sons and shall talk of them when you sit in your house and when you walk by the way and when you lie down and when you rise up. . . . And you shall write them on the doorposts of your house and on your gates." Determined to obey this command to the letter, we had followed a strategic plan to saturate each child with Christian teaching. The first music we taught them was hymns and gospel choruses. Their first stories came from the Bible. On every trip to the zoo we talked about God, the Creator. At Christmas time we made construction-paper crèches and bookmarks with pasted-on mangers and stars. We took pride in their early achievements with Scripture memorization and prayer.

We had also shared with them our well-ingrained philosophy that the only worthy goal in life was active Christian service. In one place, this had meant total family involvement in neighborhood Bible classes. With the typical exuberance of childhood, Martha, Tim, and Mary Jane had invited their friends, helped me with little details of class preparation, prayed for the success of the clubs, even shared their faith.

I recalled with special pride their concern for one neighbor who would not let his children attend our classes. After praying for several weeks for the uncooperative father, they decided to do something. One morning all three paid him a visit. When he opened the door, they handed him a piece of paper on which Martha had printed in first grade scrawl: "Believe on the Lord Jesus Christ, and thou shalt be saved" (Acts 16:31, KJV).

While we still lived in that place, a woman on a local Christian radio station interviewed me concerning my

Bible classes. She asked me what I felt was the secret of child-rearing in the Christian home. Satisfied with the responsiveness of my own children to all the training we had given them, I spoke with confidence. "If parents can just show by their lives that they're excited about Jesus Christ," I told the radio audience, "their children are bound to pick up some of that enthusiasm for themselves."

Now, six years later, as I stared at the deserted table strewn with notebooks, maps, and dog-eared Bibles, my words came back to torment me. Where had we failed? Had we, the parents, lost our enthusiasm? Our know-how? Our pied-piper charisma?

Just as the Lord had answered the desperate prayers of this parent many times before, so He spoke once more. He put a fatherly finger on first one area and then another where I had to straighten out my own thinking and begin to learn what personal, spiritual maturity was all about.

In the next few months, I became aware of His voice speaking from dozens of corners in my life—the reading nook, the social room, the prayer closet, the chapel, the family circle, and finally from our vacation spot in the redwoods.

Here, I found an ecosystem that illustrates the principle of family spiritual growth in a superb way. I discovered that the ultimate source of energy in the forest is the sun. But only the tall, adult trees can absorb the rays of the sun directly. Through the intricate interlacing of roots beneath the ground, these parent trees pass on living energy to the young saplings growing up in their shade.

Through my study of the parallels between redwood groves and families, the Lord spoke to reassure me that Walt and I had done well to saturate our children's minds with facts, memory verses, challenges, and inspirations. Thereby we had helped them to establish their own root systems. But He went on to show me that we were no longer nourishing small, tender saplings. Our children had grown tall enough and mature enough to begin reaching toward the sunshine for themselves.

Once we had glimpsed this new dimension of spiritual growth, exciting things began to happen in our home. The children asked for new Bibles. "We need a translation we can understand," they explained.

The next January, Tim announced his intention to read through his new, paraphrased Bible within the year. Remembering my own poor record with such ventures, I gave him a month or two to fizzle out. Then I watched, amazed, as two, five, eight, ten months passed, and he kept on going. Often as I tucked him into bed at night, he would look up from his open Bible and exclaim, "Mom, did you know this?"

Then he would share with me some exciting discovery he had made. December 31, our persistent son closed his Bible at the end of Revelation 22. He had made it, all on his own. And in his daily life, we noted encouraging evidences that the sun's rays he had received directly had been effectively absorbed into his growing root system.

Although all three children continued to act like normal youngsters with respect to problems, weaknesses, and mini-rebellions, we detected the gradual emergence of some personal growth patterns.

Mary Jane had for some time been a reluctant churchgoer. Now she demonstrated a new eagerness to attend. When her best friend asked, "How come you have to go to church so often?" she replied, "I go because I want to. It's fun. You ought to go with me."

In school, Martha began to stand up for her faith. When one girl approached her with the question, "How come you're so polite?" she answered without hesitation, "Because I'm a Christian, and Jesus wants me to be polite."

One of the most rewarding moments of my mothering

came several years after that awful night when I had been forced to pack away the Bible survey notebooks and begin to allow for some independent growth. Except for Martha, the family members were all in bed. She was visiting with a friend on the kitchen telephone. Walt had already fallen asleep, and I was mentally reviewing with the Lord the events of my day.

Suddenly, I became aware that Martha was nearly shouting in the other room. Without success, I tried to continue my private meditation and above all not to eavesdrop. But my bedroom door stood ajar just a crack. And resounding above my quiet thoughts came the voice of an enthusiastic teenager telling her friend, "I'm really excited about knowing Jesus Christ!"

My skin prickled into gooseflesh. "Dear God," I prayed, "she's excited about *You! Maybe her parents didn't fail too miserably after all."

As all three children finally came into their teens, we learned to enjoy them at increasingly mature levels. We found ourselves praying with David, "Let our sons in their youth be as grown-up plants, and our daughters as corner pillars fashioned as for a palace" (Psalm 144:12).

However, as the Lord answered our prayer we did not quite know how to accept the speed with which some things happened.

At fifteen, Tim was elected president of the church's high school youth council. Just after he turned sixteen, he was appointed by our youth pastor to serve as chairman of the annual Youth Week committee. Walt and I reacted with skepticism to this latter move. We knew he had done a lot of growing in the past year. We had been thrilled when, some months earlier, he had asked for a Bible translation to replace his simple paraphrase. "I need one I can use for deep Bible study," he had explained. "I want to dig out for myself the kind of riches our youth speakers share with us."

But what did a high school sophomore know about running a youth program? Surely they could have found a college student who was more mature spiritually to lead this event.

As the committee members met to lay out their plans, and our boy came home to report their progress, he made us realize that he was more mature than we had suspected. Then one afternoon I found Tim in his room. His bed was strewn with commentaries, his new study Bible, and my exhaustive concordance.

"What you up to, son?" I asked.

"Oh, I'm just getting my sermon ready," he replied with his typical, disarming casualness.

"What sermon?" I asked.

"The one I'm going to preach on Youth Sunday." Again casually.

"Oh, how nice!" I exclaimed. "They gave you a chance to preach in the evening service."

"I didn't say the evening service, Mom," he corrected me. "I'm speaking in the morning."

My pride turned to panic. Who ever heard of letting a sixteen-year-old boy deliver his first sermon in a Sunday morning worship service, Youth Sunday or no?

With effort, I swallowed a gulp and, hoping he wouldn't see how shaken I was, I said, "Well, praise the Lord."

For the next three weeks, I prayed and vacillated between proud excitement and protective dread. What if our youth pastor had made a mistake in letting Tim do this thing before he was ready? Public speaking was not his strongest point, though he had been working hard on it. He insisted that he had something important to say. But could he say it effectively? Would he fail and become discouraged? I even indulged in the folly of worrying about what the rest of the church might think of me if he did less than a polished job.

I longed to sit down with my son and help him outline his thoughts, give him a list of Scripture texts, share some poignant illustrations with him.

"I think I need some help," he confided to me one afternoon. "But not yours, Mom. This is my sermon. I want it to be new to you when you hear it."

On Youth Sunday, as Walt and I sat through the worship service, our minds were overpowered by an odd mixture of excitement, concern, and curiosity. Then Tim entered the pulpit and adjusted the tiny lapel mike around his neck. Struggling to keep my emotions from showing, I sat rigidly in my chair. I glanced sideways at Walt, who was doing the same thing. I wondered if my face betrayed my inner feelings as much as his did.

We listened, relieved and delighted, as Tim delivered his sermon with the casual poise that characterizes all he ever does. His ideas echoed faintly some things we had taught him in his sheltered days in the family grove. But we sensed a freshness about them. They were his now, shared in his own way, and gleaned from his own experiences of basking in the sunlight of direct, personal fellowship with God.

The service over, we headed home to sort out our emotions and to reassess the status of the family's spiritual maturity. Once more we were forced by our teenagers to recognize that growth had changed our family grove into a group of adult trees. True, the trunks of the younger members were not so full of rings or protective capacity as ours. And we could only imagine what the future holds of attacks by drought, disease, flood, fire, or cold. But because we stand together, roots interlaced, we can prepare to face whatever comes. As we go on growing, swaying in the breeze, lifting up branches to the sun, absorbing energy, we are confident that "He who began a good work in [us] will perfect it until the day of Jesus Christ" (Philippians 1:6).

19

Are We There Yet, Daddy?

About fifteen minutes out of San Antonio, enroute to California, we were speeding along the highway into the dusking, sunset sky. Martha popped her head up from the back seat and asked, "Are we almost there, Daddy?"

Walt and I suppressed our giggles, and he answered, "No, no, dear. We have to drive all night while you sleep. When you wake up in the morning, we'll drive all day long until it gets dark again. Then we'll drive while you sleep one more night. When you wake up that time, we'll drive for awhile longer. Then we'll be there."

"Oh." Our first grader grunted and lay down in the back seat with the other two.

All remained quiet for about fifteen more minutes. The western sky had turned to gray now, when I felt the pressure of a tiny hand gripping the back of my seat. Clearly the hopeful voice came once more. "Are we there yet, Daddy?"

On that long trip home for a family reunion, our little ones reminded us that concepts of time and distance lie beyond the comprehension of a child. On subsequent trips, they have shown a progressive ability to grasp these basic facts. Today when we start out for Disneyland, they know very well what eight hours of sitting is going to mean. In fact, their turn has even come to help with the driving.

Similarly, trekking through life with these same children has shown us that a reasonable understanding of what it means to reach our growing-up destination also develops slowly.

In junior high school all three of our children enjoyed one special English teacher. One night, following a Christmas concert at the school, our whole family visited for a long while with the teacher and her husband. Several days later, Martha brought home a Christmas card from that same teacher. Inside was a note: "To the Herrs, a beautiful example of 'family.' "

At that point, I glowed with the pride of accomplishment and began to ask the Lord, "Are we there yet, Father?"

My answer came on a hectic morning soon thereafter. The alarm had not gone off. I had forgotten to take my homemade bread out of the freezer the night before so I could slice it for sandwiches. Wearing a bathrobe and with hair stringy, I dashed about the kitchen in an effort to put breakfast on the table and create a substitute for sandwiches, while the girls fought over the bathroom, and Tim loitered in bed. Tempers flared, everybody missed the school bus, and Walt was late for work because he had to wait for the kids to get ready so he could take them to school.

When I had finally chased out the door the last sleepy-eyed child, shoes and socks still in hand, I collapsed into the rocking chair. Between sips of strong, black coffee, I sighed, "What ever happened to our beautiful example of family?"

No, we had not arrived yet. In fact, with the passing of the years, I have concluded that we will never fully arrive. Always, just when I think things are under control, somebody throws the switch that turns on confusion. Once more we are brought face to face with the immaturities in all of us—and in our family as a unit.

As I have looked around me in the community and in the church, I have observed two kinds of families. First, I have seen a large number of scattered, unhappy homes—households of isolated persons who do not like themselves and who cannot relate to one another. But I have also discovered a lot of warm, growing homes, where all is not perfect but where love seems to hold everything together. Through these observations, I began to suspect that God does intend us to reach a point of relative maturity, where life takes on a stabilized character.

Then I read what instruction the Scripture had given for building toward this maturity: "Let us, therefore, keep before us whatever will contribute to peace and the development of one another" (Romans 14:19, Goodspeed*). I concluded that, yes, relative maturity must be possible.

Again, I asked the Lord: "But what about us? Are we there yet, Father?"

I was aware that in recent weeks things had not been too smooth on the home front. Extra pressures came with the building of our house addition, adjusting to some changes in life-style, adding two new drivers (while totaling the second car), and coping with external problems that involved the whole family. All of these, along with each person's individual pressure points and growth pains, were contributing to tension in the family circle. As I fought my way through a tight web of personal hindrances to stability, I sought for some evidence of the relative maturity I hoped might still be ours.

About this time, Martha decided to attend a Christian writers' conference with me. She had talked about it before, but I never took her too seriously. Now, when the way opened so that she could go, she jumped at the chance. Eagerly, she made all the necessary arrangements to be away from school for the week.

One morning I asked her, "Martha, why do you really

*Edgar Johnson Goodspeed, *The New Testament: An American Translation.*

want to go with me? I know you're interested in writing and in meeting new people. But many young people wouldn't think of going to such a conference with their mothers."

My enthusiastic teenager reached out and took my hand in hers. With a contented smile, she said, "Mom, you've allowed me to make many of my own decisions in the past few years. So, when I'm given the choice, there's nobody I'd rather do things with than you." She went on to explain how she appreciated being able to share an experience. Yet, she knew I would let her be on her own when she wanted or needed to be, so as to learn for herself what the Lord planned to give her through the conference.

"Thank you, Father," I prayed. Here was the evidence of relative maturity I had sought. In my mind, I gathered more bits and pieces of evidence to complete the picture. And I realized that ours is a family where three and sometimes even four generations share life in a hundred areas. We play and work together, laugh and cry together, talk and listen, share deep thoughts, keep special secrets, care about one another while respecting each person's privacy, pray and serve together.

Day after day, in the excitement of family living, we are helping each other on toward our goal of maturity. In the process, we are experiencing the delight that comes from knowing that growing up is a family affair.

Notes

CHAPTER 3

1. James Dobson, *Hide or Seek* (Old Tappan, N.J.: Revell, 1974), p. 60.

CHAPTER 4

1. Gladys Hunt, *Honey for a Child's Heart* (Grand Rapids: Zondervan, 1969), p. 60.

CHAPTER 5

1. Eileen Guder, *God, but I'm Bored* (Garden City, N.J.: Doubleday, 1971), p. 23.

CHAPTER 7

1. Reuel Howe, *The Creative Years* (Greenwich, Conn.: Seabury, 1959), p. 136.
2. Ibid., p. 137.

CHAPTER 8

1. Raymond Rogers, *Coming into Existence: The Struggle to Become an Individual* (Cleveland: World, 1967), pp. 9-10.

CHAPTER 13

1. Bruce Larson, *Living on the Growing Edge* (Grand Rapids: Zondervan, 1968), p. 46.

CHAPTER 16

1. Paul Tournier, *Secrets* (Richmond: Knox, 1963), pp. 22-23.

CHAPTER 17

1. Paul Tournier, *Secrets* (Richmond: Knox, 1963), pp. 22-23.

Moody Press, a ministry of the Moody Bible Institute, is designed for education, evangelization, and edification. If we may assist you in knowing more about Christ and the Christian life, please write us without obligation: Moody Press, c/o MLM, Chicago, Illinois 60610.